BUSINESS IDIOMS INTERNATIONAL

Other ESP titles of interest include:

Adamson, D.
*Starting English for Business**

Brieger, N. and J. Comfort
*Developing Business Contacts**

Brieger, N. and J. Comfort
*Advanced Business Contacts**

Brieger, N. and A. Cornish
*Secretarial Contacts**

Brieger, N. and J. Comfort
*Technical Contacts**

Brieger, N. and J. Comfort
*Social Contacts**

Brieger, N. and J. Comfort
Business Issues

Brieger, N. and Sweeney, S.
The Language of Business English

Davies, S. et al.
*Bilingual Handbooks of Business
Correspondence and Communication*

Minkoff, P.
Executive Skills

Palstra, R.
*Telephone English**

Business Management English Series

Comfort, J. and N. Brieger
Marketing

Comfort, J. and N. Brieger
Finance

Brieger, N. and J. Comfort
Production and Operations

Brieger, N. and J. Comfort
Personnel

* Includes audio cassette(s)

BUSINESS IDIOMS

INTERNATIONAL

CHRISTOPHER GODDARD

PHOENIX
ELT

incorporating
PRENTICE HALL MACMILLAN

New York London Toronto Sydney Tokyo Singapore

Published 1995 by
Phoenix ELT
Campus 400, Spring Way
Maylands Avenue, Hemel Hempstead
Hertfordshire, HP2 7EZ
A division of Prentice Hall International

First published 1994 by Prentice Hall International

© International Book Distributors Ltd

Typeset in Melior and Univers by
Fakenham Photosetting Ltd

Printed and bound in Great Britain by
The Bath Press, Bath.

Library of Congress Cataloging-in-Publication Data

Goddard, Christopher.
    Business idioms international / Christopher Goddard.
        p. cm.
    Includes index.
    ISBN 0–13–042490–0
    1. English language – Conversation and phrase books
    (for merchants)
    2. English language – Business English.   3. English
    language – Idioms.
    4. Business – Terminology.   I. Title.
PE1115.G58   1993
428.3'4'02465 – dc20   93–6189
                                                              CIP

British Library Cataloguing in Publication Data

A catalogue record for this book is available from
the British Library

ISBN 0–13–042490–0
    5 96

Acknowledgements

The author and publisher are grateful to 'The Mail on Sunday' for permission to reproduce the article on pp 114.

Note: The concept of Auto Security Net and any figures or statistics used in this book to support it are purely imaginative and illustrative.

For *FUJIKO*

Thanks to my son Nick who came up with the storyline and the ending. To Isobel Fletcher de Téllez who checked the book over in detail as it took shape, to make sure that the end product isn't a complete dud! To colleagues and students whose helpful comments have made this book possible and to whom I may conveniently pass the buck if it isn't an instant best-seller!

Contents

Introduction

An idiom is:

- a short and effective way of expressing ideas and attitudes in words
- a combination of words, working as a team with its own energy, its own special meaning; a meaning separate and different from the sum of the single words from which it is formed, in the same way as a chemical compound is different from a simple mixture

This book contains 350 sentence, clause, phrase and phrasal verb idioms, including noun or adjective forms where they exist. These idioms have been carefully chosen from over 10,000 studied, to reflect those most used in a business and professional situation whenever English is used as the common language of communication. Whereas the world of business has its own phraseology – even jargon – this book reflects the fact that many of its idioms are the same as those used frequently in a non-business setting.

MAIN FEATURES OF 'BUSINESS IDIOMS'

The intention of this book is to provide a selection of the most useful, most international and least confusing idioms to lighten the learning-load for a learner of English. The features that have guided the making of the book and the choice of idioms to be included are discussed below.

1. Every English-speaking country has different kinds of language for different purposes and for different occasions, for example: written and spoken language; 'street' language and slang; informal, neutral and formal language; specialist technical language and so on. One problem facing speakers of English as a second or foreign language, is to avoid being either too formal or too informal and to avoid using an inappropriate form of language (for example, using the language of poetry to describe a scientific process or using street language during an important meeting). So, the first and main feature of this book is that **it provides a range of idioms which**, with a few exceptions (clearly marked *informal*), **can safely be used on almost any occasion** from discussions and meetings to presentations, negotiations, reports and letters.

2. The second feature of this book is that all the idioms can be used wherever English is spoken, whether as a first, second or foreign language. For this reason, the idioms are not linked to any limited or specific areas of life or

culture in English-speaking countries. (The few sporting idioms are included because sport is international.) In other words, these idioms are not simply 'English' English idioms or 'American' English idioms or idioms of any other type of English which can only easily be used and understood by native speakers of those countries. Although the idioms represented in this book, may have originated in a particular language community, **the idioms can be used and understood by English speakers worldwide**.

3. Since the purpose of language is clear communication of information and ideas, **this book focuses on idioms which are not likely to be misunderstood or confused with other idioms** (confusion is a common problem, especially in the case of some phrasal verbs with several different meanings). For that reason, a number of well-known idioms have not been included. In particular, phrasal verb idioms in this book are limited to those with a single or usual meaning (in the latter case any secondary meanings are clearly marked).

4. The language of idioms comes naturally to native speakers, but for those whose native language is not English, it can be a problem to find the right words at the right time. For this reason **the idioms are arranged in units with functional headings** to make it easier to find the right words at the right time and for the right purpose. These functional headings appear in the Contents, together with a list of the idioms to be found under that heading. These headings will help you to identify the area of meaning that you need. When you find an idiom in a text or tapescript that you wish to look up, the index at the back of the book will help you to find it.

WHO IS 'BUSINESS IDIOMS' FOR?

Although it may be of some interest to native speakers, this book is primarily for users of English as an international language who have reached at least intermediate level. In particular, it is for those in business and other commercial areas who need to communicate clearly and powerfully in day-to-day transactions.

MAIN COMPONENTS OF 'BUSINESS IDIOMS'

The study units

Each unit contains a number of idioms, linked to a common function. A definition of each idiom is provided. Definitions are followed by several example sentences which illustrate both the meaning and the syntactical possibilities of the idiom. In these examples the idiom being defined appears in italics. Each idiom appears at least four times throughout the book. This reinforcement is essential to the learning process, and demonstrates just how naturally and frequently these idioms occur in many contexts. A reinforced (or anticipated) idiom is indicated by underlining. The idioms also occur repeatedly in the Practice Sections, but for practical reasons cannot be underlined, because they are so numerous. In addition to the 350 featured idioms, many further useful expressions which appear in the examples are later reintroduced in the Practice Sections.

The Study Units do not, and cannot, claim to constitute a dictionary; the number and scope of idioms included here is simply not large or wide enough. Indeed, one major strength of the book lies in the fact that the idioms in it have been selected from a whole corpus, so that, with its deliberately specific functional range it contains only relevant practical idioms for professional use.

The practice sections

After every four units there is a Practice Section.

In general, idioms from each group of four Study Units are practised in the Practice Section immediately following. On the other hand, idioms and expressions in the Practice Sections are not limited to those from previous Study Units. This is partly to avoid artificial limitations on the use of language, and partly because one of the aims of this book is to make the student familiar with the idioms contained in it both by anticipation and by reinforcement.

Within the Practice Sections, a realistic business project is described and its progress followed through from its early stages towards production. The storyline is presented through both reading and listening texts. As you follow the storyline you encounter people, situations, memos, presentations, letters, and so on where idioms are used, and reused, as a matter of course, in order to get a job done. By doing the tasks and exercises you not only practise the idioms, but move forward with the business project. Each Practice Section deals with a particular business area, as you will see from the section titles in the Contents.

The Practice Sections contain exercises in reading, listening, speaking and writing so that you encounter the idioms and use them yourself in situations in which they naturally occur. There are several Word Study exercises in each Practice Section where further expressions, including many from the Study Units, appear in addition to the idioms being practised.

Tapescripts

It may be useful for you to read the tapescripts of the recorded material. These contain many examples of idioms featured in this book. These idioms are set in italics for easy identification. This will help you to see how naturally and frequently they are used.

In addition, reading the tapescripts and listening to the cassette at the same time will help overcome problems of pronouncing expressions and, in particular, of identifying them when you hear them. This will be especially useful to those with a major problem arising from difficulty in making the connection between written and spoken English.

Answer key

This is provided for you to check your answers and will be especially helpful if you are working alone.

Index

This is a useful reference resource to help you locate the definition of an idiom. It has been prepared with a view to easy reference, so that checking the meaning of an idiom anywhere in the book can be done quickly and efficiently. For example, in the tapescript for Question 3 in Practice Section A, you will see the idiom *action we're going to take*. This idiom (*to take action*) can be found under both 'take' and 'action' in the index. Most of the idioms in this book can be found in the same way, by looking in more than one place in the index.

HOW TO USE THIS BOOK

As we have seen, this book is not a dictionary. Also, it is not simply a 'book of idioms', but a flexible course in practical business and professional communication, complete in itself. It incorporates the many essential idioms, which are often used but rarely taught.

If you want to use this book as a reference resource, with a view to active communication in English, you will find it useful as long as you have a general idea of what you want to say. So if, for example, you are going to take part in a negotiation, you can look at Study Units 18 to 28 and Practice Sections F and G where you will find many expressions which may be useful for that purpose. If, on the other hand, you simply need to check the meaning of an English idiom not contained in this book, you need a dictionary.

It is important to remember that, in essence, this book is a practice book (the Practice Sections) with a specialised reference section (the Study Units) and you will get most benefit from it by using it as such, whether you are working alone or with a teacher. Probably the best way of all to use this book is as a functional course book in effective business and professional communication in English, with incidental grammar and lexical input but with a practical focus. In that case it would make sense to start at the beginning and work in sequence through each group of four Study Units, followed by a Practice Section, so that you study Practice Sections A–G in order and follow the storyline bit by bit.

However, in case this is not possible or needed, the Practice Sections have been arranged so that each is self-contained. That is to say, each Practice Section focuses on one area of business. In addition the storyline is updated in brief at the beginning of each Practice Section in order to put that section in perspective with regard to the story as a whole. This is particularly useful if you are joining a group after the start of a course or if the book is to be used in part only as supplementary material for a main course.

Speaking Generally

as a rule usually (but not always)

- I don't *as a rule* interview clients after five o'clock, although I do make an exception for urgent cases.
- *As a rule* we deliver within seven days of receipt of order.
- We prefer payment in $US or DM *as a rule*.

as usual as always; in the normal or accustomed way; following a normal pattern

- An annual bonus will be paid *as usual* to employees who have performed well this year.
- The bank will be pleased to offer your company a loan or overdraft facility. *As usual*, the directors will be asked to sign the necessary documents.

the exception proves the rule something which differs from the usual, the normal, or some principle, rule or theory and yet, by the same token, reinforces what is usual etc. [Also **an exception to the rule** someone or something which differs from the usual, the normal or some principle, rule or theory*].

- Bankers will confirm that most customers are honest and repay their loans on time; put differently, the relatively few fraudsters and bad payers are *the exceptions that prove the rule*.
- *Tests have shown that this product lasts at least three times longer than other similar products, so it is quite *an exception to the rule*.

for the most part mainly; generally; largely; in the majority of cases or instances; on the whole.

- That's an interesting idea. *For the most part* I agree with you, but I have my doubts about a couple of points.
- Our clients are not rich, *for the most part*.
- *For the most part*, staff remain with the company for at least five years.

to hold good to continue to be consistently or constantly correct, true, valid or applicable [Also **to hold true***]

- Does the offer you made last week still *hold good*?
- The conditions which gave rise to easy profits over the last three years no longer *hold good*.
- *Some scientific and other principles established over 2,000 years ago still *hold true* today.

in general/in particular speaking generally (followed by a specific example or, especially) [Note: *In general* and *in particular* may be used together or separately – see examples]

- Today, I'd like us to consider marketing *in general* and European marketing *in particular*.
- Our main competitor is trying to drive everyone else – and us *in particular* – out of the market.
- We do not, *in general*, like our office staff to come to work wearing jeans.

in principle as a general idea or principle, but without considering details or practical possibilities [Note: *In principle* is occasionally used as an adjective as in an *in-principle* decision]

- So, *in principle*, then, we are agreed on the new proposals. We now have to study them in depth before reaching a final decision.
- I can say, 'yes', *in principle*, now, as long as you understand that this is subject to checking that importing your product is not against our import regulations.

in theory/in practice what should be correct, according to some rule or principle, in contrast with the actual situation [Note: *in theory* and *in practice* may be used separately*]

- *In theory* this machine could be converted to run on a different fuel, although *in practice* this would be expensive.
- *Yes, we work hard – the office is open until 1700 although *in practice* everyone goes home at 1800.
- *In practice*, equality exists only as a mathematical phenomenon.

nine times out of ten almost always

- *Nine times out of ten* our customers are completely satisfied.

- If you want to reach me between 1900 and 2000, *nine times out of ten* you'll find me at the Cafe Espejo in Recoletos.

no exception or **(not) any exception** thing or person following or forming part of some expected or normal type, pattern or rule

- The last few years have been difficult ones for the company. As we have seen from the latest annual report and accounts, last year proved *no exception*.
- The notice says, 'Helmets must be worn on the construction site'. I take it that you can read, but you're not wearing a helmet – so what makes you think you're *any exception*?

on paper in theory; if judged from the written evidence

- The new printed circuit board design looks good *on paper*, however, it remains to be seen whether it will work in reality.
- According to its brochure, the company has offices in 15 countries, so *on paper* it's a well-established multinational.
- Both candidates have excellent CVs, so they're promising *on paper*; what we have to do is judge their potential performance at interview.

on the whole generally speaking; considering the most important or the majority of factors [Same as for the most part]

- *On the whole*, last year was successful, with profits up by eight per cent in spite of difficulties in the market.
- It seems a good idea, but I think *on the whole* I'd prefer not to make an immediate decision. It's an important matter and I'd like to reflect on it, in case I have second thoughts.

The Nature of Things

as such in or by its nature; considered alone; (in) itself [Also means in that capacity or function]

- The process *as such* is simple in concept, although the machinery required to operate it is highly complex.
- The company *as such* is in a strong financial position; the group as a whole, however, is not.
- He had recently been promoted to sales manager and felt that, *as such*, he ought to have two secretaries.

to consist of to be made (up) of; to be composed of; to comprise

- Water *consists of* two parts of hydrogen to one part of oxygen.
- 'How many people does the negotiating team *consist of*?'
  'Three – the Sales Director plus two experts.'

in itself standing or taken alone or separately; viewed or considered by itself as a thing isolated or apart from other things

- Hard work is *in itself* not enough to guarantee success – skill, luck, an ability to get on with people and other factors all play a part.
- Each stage of the process *in itself* produces only a limited effect but in aggregate the results are impressive.
- The design of this product is exceptional *in itself*. That, and its performance and durability, should guarantee it a market.

in the nature of being similar in type or character to; rather like

- Although the wording of the letter was polite, it was nonetheless clearly *in the nature of* a threat.
- Our products are *in the nature of* accessories to a lifestyle which few can afford.
- The rise and fall of share prices can be seen *in the nature of* a thermometer of market confidence.

in (its) own right because of what it is as such or in itself and independent of any other relationship

- Bangladesh, once part of Pakistan, has for some years been a country *in its own right*.
- Not content with being merely the husband of a successful woman, he became successful *in his own right* as a journalist.
- Our managing director's authority stems from his outstanding personal qualities *in their own right*, more than from his official capacity as such.

in the shape of specifically; in the form of; in particular; namely (followed by details of something general)

- The government is expected to introduce new economic measures *in the shape of* laws to do with tax, privatisation and import controls.
- We can arrange finance for you, *in the shape of* a loan for the required amount, repayable at fifteen per cent, per annum over five years, secured against the company premises.
- The research and development department needs new facilities *in the shape of* a larger workshop and better equipment.

of (its) own accord spontaneously; as a result of ones's own action, will or decision and not because of some outside influence or action

- It would be better if the chairman resigned *of his own accord*, rather than as a result of pressure from the board.
- The company decided *of its own accord*, without consultation with the unions, to close the plant and transfer production elsewhere.
- We can do this the easy way or the hard way – in a word, either you follow company regulations *of your own accord* or your stay with the company will be a short one. I hope I have made myself crystal clear.

3

STUDY UNIT

Connection

according to following; corresponding to; in relation to; as said by; depending on

- The foreman was disciplined *according to* the rules laid down for the offence.
- Sales representatives are paid an annual bonus *according to* the number and value of units sold over a certain minimum.
- *According to* the financial press, your company's share price has fallen due to poor trading results. Do you agree with this assessment?
- If our journey goes *according to* plan, we should be in Pretoria on Friday.

in accordance with following the terms or requirements of; (acting) in conformity with; as stated by; in line with

- Payment must be made within twenty-eight days, *in accordance with* the contract.
- The government's plans to increase taxes are not *in accordance with* its election manifesto.
- *In accordance with* your instructions contained in telex of 09 March, we have today despatched 250 inflatable boats, model 'Désirée'.

as to about; regarding

- That's all about our general objectives. Next, *as to* putting together a game plan for reaching these objectives, can I have some ideas, please?
- We have to weigh up the pros and cons – *as to* the risks on the one hand and the opportunities on the other.

to do with connected with; related to [Also **got to do with***]

- I'd like to speak to the production department; it's *to do with* our order for spare parts.
- These ideas are very interesting, but they have nothing *to do with* what we are discussing.
- *Yes, I know the pound is down against the deutschmark, but what has that *got to do with* the fact that your contract payment is late?

hand in hand working together or as a team; in conjunction with; as a complement to [Note: *hand in hand* could be used as an adjective as in *hand-in-hand* collaboration]

- The news that some politicians were working *hand in hand* with organised crime brought about a scandal.
- On this project, we'll be working *hand-in-hand* with our overseas partners.
- Inflation goes *hand in hand* with demands for wage increases.

in conjunction (with) operating, functioning, working, acting or planning together; in collaboration

- On this project, you'll be working *in conjunction with* two other departments.
- The two machines work *in conjunction with* each other to obtain the result.
- The finance department and the legal department are working *in conjunction* on the new share issue.

in connection (with) about, concerning, relating or relevant to

- I'm phoning *in connection with* your letter of the sixth of September.
- We're now going to examine projected staffing levels. *In that connection*, I'd like you to look at this chart.
- We seem to have reached agreement on financial matters. I now want to talk to you *in another connection*.

to refer to to have connection with; to direct attention to [Also means to formally transfer from one authority to another*]

- The new policy *refers to* both office and factory workers.
- What I am going to say is important and *refers to* all of us.
- Yesterday, we discussed the new process in general. Today, I'm going to *refer to* some of its details.
- *In connection with your request for a purchase order I must *refer* you *to* our Customer Services department.

in terms of by taking as an example of; concerning; with regard to

- *In terms of* quality, our products are second to none.
- The new system, although more expensive to operate, is better *in terms of* efficiency.
- The costs of the earthquake can be counted *in terms of* billions, rather than millions, of dollars.
- The government has made its position clear *in terms of* its industrial policy.

on behalf of as representative or spokesman for

- I shall be attending the meeting tomorrow *on behalf of* the finance director, who is unwell.
- *On* the company*'s behalf*, I would like to thank all personnel for their performance this year. This has produced excellent results, as we have seen from the trading figures.
- I know you've more or less decided to dismiss your assistant, but before you do, I'd like to say a few words *on* his *behalf*.

(in) touch with in contact by the spoken or written word
to be in touch to be in contact
to get in touch to make contact
to keep or **stay in touch** to continue contact
to lose touch to lose contact
out of touch not in contact [Note: *out of touch* is normally used, by extension, as a criticism*; also note the expression out of touch with reality – example in Study Unit 21]

- Although they don't see each other very often, they are *in* constant *touch* by letter or phone.
- As soon as we have a response from our agents in Seoul, we'll *get in touch with* you by fax or phone at once.
- Goodbye, let's *keep in touch* and if the chance comes up, maybe we can do business some time in the future.
- We *stay in touch with* stock exchange movements worldwide, with a view to providing a better service for our clients.
- No, we haven't heard from our agents in Brazil for some time; we *lost touch* when they moved their office.
- *I'm afraid this scheme is totally *out of touch with* current developments in the electronics industry.

with regard to concerning; regarding; in connection with; in terms of; referring to

- If you meet us half way *with regard to* price, then we can consider placing a bigger order.
- 'Why does the boss want to see me?' 'In all probability, *with regard to* your sales for April.'
- In connection with the contract terms, we can agree to the first three points.

With regard to the remainder, these are not in accordance with what was agreed on at our meeting.
- Now, *with regard to* these investment proposals, in my opinion they seem well thought out and we won't be running too many risks by going along with them.
- Although the new motor is clearly a breakthrough in engine technology, as yet it's too early to start planning *with regard* to large scale production.

4 Cause and Effect

STUDY UNIT

to arise from to originate from; to be due to; to be caused by
- Misunderstandings often *arise from* language problems.
- The confusion about the date of the meeting *arose from* a typing error.

to bring about to cause; to make (something) happen; to give rise to
- The discovery of more efficient methods *brought about* major changes on the production line.
- Careful planning of objectives, strategy and tactics are necessary *to bring about* a successful negotiation.

to give rise to to cause; to bring about
- Bad trading conditions generally *give rise to* an increase in bankruptcies.
- Poor trading figures *gave rise to* a fall in share prices.

to have an effect or **impact on** to affect; to influence
- Rising imports *have had a* considerable *effect on* our balance of payments.
- The election result *had an* immediate *impact on* share prices.
- Improved working conditions *had* only *a* marginal *effect on* production: what the workforce really wanted was a pay rise.

to result in to be (or have as) the result [Note: **to result from** means to be (or have as) the cause*]
- The experiment *resulted in* success.
- Our present policy will clearly *result in* losses.
- *We hope that some progress *will result from* our discussion.

to stem from to originate from; to be caused by
- Company losses *stemmed from* poor management.
- Her success in politics *stems from* hard work and intelligence.

to trigger off to cause or bring about (an important or serious effect, often negative, sudden or violent) [Also **to spark off**; **to touch off***]
- The advertising film about the new car *triggered off* an enormous public response, so that demand for the product was greater than supply.
- *The management decision *sparked off* a series of damaging strikes.
- *The invention of the petrol engine *touched off* a revolution in transport.

A

PRACTICE

The Planning Meeting

STORYLINE

Boldmere PLC is a medium-sized, independently operating British subsidiary of a US company involved in the design and production of electronic security systems.

The company has invented a system which gives cars and other vehicles an electronic link to a network of detection centres. *In effect*, this would make it possible to trace any vehicle fitted with the device.

Boldmere has obtained a provisional patent to protect its invention. Although protection operates worldwide, it is limited to eighteen months. During that time, the company has the sole right to develop, manufacture and market the system, so it is free of competition. However, at the end of the protection period, competitors are free to do as they wish.

The company can try to obtain full patents worldwide, *in order to* extend the protection period. But *in practice* this is a long and expensive process, with no guarantee of success.

❶ WARM-UP

What advice would you give to Boldmere at this stage about how to proceed with the development of their invention?

❷ WORD STUDY

What is the meaning of the words/expressions below which are used in the storyline and in the meeting you are about to hear? Show that you know the meaning by practising using them in short sentences.

a. subsidiary
b. involved
c. link
d. detection
e. trace
f. vehicle
g. provision
h. patent
i. sole

j. diversify
k. prioritise
l. resources
m. run out
n. Are you with me?
o. the finished product
p. the crux of the matter
q. in point of fact
r. without more ado

❸ LISTENING • COMPREHENSION

 Boldmere holds a board meeting, attended by Jack Wagner, Chief Executive, Julia Van der Merwe, Marketing Director, and Norman Buchan, Finance Director, to discuss the position. Listen to an extract from the meeting at Boldmere's offices. Then answer the following questions.

a. What is the purpose of the meeting?

b. What does Van der Merwe say is the most important thing to do?

c. What reason does she give?

d. What attitude does Buchan show to Van der Merwe's opinion?

e. What reasons does he give?

f. What does he say is the most important thing to do?

g. What reason(s) does he give?

h. Does Wagner think that the answer must be EITHER Van der Merwe's OR Buchan's opinion?

❹ WORD STUDY

Match the half sentences on the left with the correct other half on the right to make a simple sentence. The first is done for you.

a. I can't make up my mind	**1.** the machinery started to go wrong.
b. What action should we take	**2.** to resolve this problem?
c. I don't follow you. What	**3.** to plan ahead.
d. I want an answer straight away,	**4.** are you aiming at?
e. It makes sense	**5.** that tax has to be paid.
f. The fact of the matter is	**6.** all this work; it's too much.
g. Production ran smoothly until	**7.** not next week.
h. I can't cope with	**8.** whether to do it or not.

❺ TRANSFER

What possible solutions do you think Jack Wagner is likely to propose?

❻ WORD STUDY

On the left are some expressions used in the meeting. All of them appear in this book and are listed in the index. Now look at the expressions on the right and try to find the one that is closest in meaning.

Used at the meeting	Closest in meaning
a. agree up to a point	**1.** manage or be satisfied with
b. a drawback	**2.** obvious
c. what's more	**3.** you have not taken all the important factors into account
d. take first place	**4.** it is true
e. run up against	**5.** a disadvantage or problem
f. smooth out	**6.** I agree partly but I'm not saying how much.
g. taking steps to	**7.** I respect your opinion which may be right
h. I take your point	**8.** supposing
i. as far as it goes	**9.** is the most important priority
j. what if ... ?	**10.** trying to/taking action to
k. crystal clear	**11.** meet
l. to make do with	**12.** and this is another reason
m. in fact	**13.** to resolve/deal with

❼ LISTENING • NOTE-TAKING

 Listen to the second part of the board meeting. Take notes about what Jack Wagner proposes and the problems Julia Van der Merwe and Norman Buchan raise.

❽ WORD STUDY

On the left is a list of some of the idioms used at the meeting. They can all be found in this book and in the index. Look at the expressions on the right and try to find the expression which is closest in meaning to the idiom.

Used at the meeting	Closest in meaning
a. in future	**1.** decide
b. it's a matter of	**2.** in the way described
c. so far	**3.** always after today
d. make our minds up	**4.** to find the explanation or cause
e. in reality	**5.** some time soon
f. above all	**6.** it depends on
g. get to the bottom of	**7.** earlier than originally planned
h. in the near future	**8.** one way of achieving some objective
i. in that respect	**9.** until now
j. a means to an end	**10.** during
k. in the course of	**11.** this is the most important thing
l. ahead of schedule	**12.** this is truth, not imagination

❾ COMPREHENSION QUESTIONS

a. What is Wagner's attitude towards the solutions suggested by the other two speakers?

b. Does Wagner say that the most important thing is to choose either Van der Merwe's suggestion or Buchan's suggestion?

c. Wagner goes on to summarise the important factors *on* which the company's decision must be *based*. What are these factors?

d. What is the solution proposed by Wagner?

e. What was the final result of the meeting?

❿ TRANSFER

a. Your task at this meeting was to take notes and prepare a summary. Write minutes or a memorandum, stating what was discussed, the opinions given and the result. Listen to the tape again if you need to.

b. Now, using your notes, make an oral summary. *Refer to* the tapescript if you need to.

c. How do you think Boldmere should now *go ahead*?

STORYLINE

At the next meeting of the Boldmere board, an agreement was reached, as you can see from the following memorandum.

Boldmere plc

From: Jack Wagner

To: Norman Buchan/Julia Van der Merwe

19 January

Re: ASN Marketing and Finance

In connection with Monday's meeting, it was agreed that while ASN can easily and cheaply be fitted to vehicles of all kinds, it is quite another matter to set up the supporting network of transceiver sites. In reality, installation of these is likely to take a great deal of time and money, unless we can find an alternative. Any major problems with marketing and finance will, in all probability, stem from this single all-important factor. In the same way it will have an impact on our marketing strategy. The fact that our patent protection runs out in just under eighteen months has been fully taken account of. After weighing up all the pros and cons, we agree that on balance it is taking too much of a chance simply to forge ahead on all systems go with worldwide – or even national – marketing straight away. In lieu, for the time being we are to look into ways of setting up ASN on a limited scale (most likely in a major UK city) to start with. This will also be a means to a longer-term end – with a view to demonstrating to our wider markets that we can make the system work. In that way we limit our marketing/financial risks.

This first step will require medium-term finance in the shape of loan/overdraft facilities. Any subsequent expansion would of course involve very substantial capital expenditure requiring a large-scale issue of shares/bonds.

NB has prepared a first-stage costing and cash-flow projection (copy annexed). We have all seen this and approved it so that it can now go to the bank with our proposals.

J

⑪ TRANSFER

Study the financial information supplied by Boldmere to its bankers. This *consists of* the graphics below which were prepared by Buchan and agreed by Wagner and Van der Merwe following the meeting. Consider/discuss the graphics *in order to* find the best *game plan* for marketing and financing Auto Security Net.

Costing / Price

Project AUTO SECURITY NET (ASN)

Estimated total cost over 5 years (£000s) 4, 942

Estimated 5 year production 101,000 UNITS

Unit price To be agreed, but for projection purposes fixed at minimal 50

Unit production cost 48.93

Mark-up (for projection purposes only) 1.07

ASN Cash flow forecast (£000s)					
	Yr 1	**Yr 2**	**Yr 3**	**Yr 4**	**Yr 5**
Opening cash balance		+870	+770	+929	+1332
* Capital introduced	1400				
Sales	250	750	950	1250	1850
Total receipts	1650	750	950	1250	1850
Salaries and wages	60	80	100	120	140
Components	30	100	120	150	180
Production overheads	10	15	20	25	30
Administrative overheads	6	8	10	12	15
Sales and distribution	15	15	15	15	15
Site costs	400	400	400	400	400
Equipment and machinery	20	3	3	3	3
Servicing banking facility	239	229	123	112	101
Total payments	780	850	791	827	884
Cash movements	+870	−100	+159	+413	+996
Closing cash balance	+870	+770	+929	+1332	+2308
* Includes 600 Banking facility					

⑫ TRANSFER

Read the text and answer the following questions.

Inflation in a nation's economy stems from a number of factors and has an impact on the daily lives of all citizens. It gives rise to an increase in the cost of living and, by the same token, may lower the standard of living as incomes fail to keep up with the inflationary spiral. Numerous social ills arise from inflation, for it can bring about bankruptcy and trigger off divorce, suicide and civil unrest, amongst other evils. In a word, inflation results in misery for millions.

a. Underline the expressions showing **cause** and **effect**.

b. Using some of the expressions you have underlined, explain in a few sentences the causes and effects of:
1. pollution
2. strikes (industrial action)
3. bankruptcy
4. some other positive or negative state of affairs – your choice.

Priorities

above all (else) most importantly (of all)

- We have several matters to consider. *Above all*, however, is the question of financing our new project.
- A successful managing director requires, *above all else*, a thick skin.
- Now I'd like to turn our attention to safety equipment, which, *above all*, must be kept readily available.

all important most important; urgent or necessary [Note: *all-important* can be used as an adverb or adjective*]

- Speed, surprise and superiority are *all important* as factors for success in commercial, as well as military, operations.
- *Above all, we must be as efficient and effective as our products. So, the *all-important* thing to remember is to think and act quickly and do your job well.

first and foremost firstly and most important

- At this meeting we have several matters to consider. *First and foremost* is to decide on a replacement for the production manager, who sadly died last week.
- In our discussions, I hope you will agree that *first and foremost* we should identify the common ground between our two companies and, by the same token, isolate the matters to be negotiated.
- At this, our annual dinner, I would like to welcome, *first and foremost*, our guests from overseas, also all staff and friends of the company.

(the) first step the first stage, or part, of some process or series of actions

- When making a presentation, *the first step* is to define exactly what you are going to speak about.
- Right, so this is what we're going to do. As *a first step*, we're going to improve our corporate image. We will then introduce our new product range, before targeting new markets.
- We hope that this discussion will bear fruit and so be *the first step* towards greater cooperation between us.

last but not least introducing the next item on the list, which, although the last, is not less important than the others

- We need to think about how much capital we want to raise, for what purpose and, *last but not least*, how we're going to get it.
- I'd like to thank everyone for their efforts, which have made the year such a successful one for the company – directors, managers, executives, office and factory staff and, *last but not least*, their respective wives and husbands, who play an unseen but nonetheless vital role.
- Now, coming to the end of my presentation, *the last, but* certainly *not the least*, of our options is to move our headquarters to a less expensive site, outside the capital, but keeping a small office in the city centre.

to take (first) place to be (the most) important; to have (top) priority

- Company policy should be based on the interests of the company as a whole. This must *take first place* over the interests of shareholders, managers and employees.
- Claims for compensation arising from the recent air disaster will no doubt *take first place* at today's meeting of the airline company's board.
- In the light of the company's current difficulties, cost reductions must *take first place*, at least in the short term.
- For the past few years, payment of dividends to shareholders has been very much a matter of course. However, in the present circumstances, this must now *take second place* to making headway with our investment programme.

6

STUDY UNIT

Purpose and Objective

to aim at to plan to, or to try to, reach or hit an objective, goal or target

- Our products *are aimed at* working mothers.
- The manager's critical remarks about inefficiency *were aimed at* the chairman.
- This experiment *aims at* showing how to measure the volume of water.

the aim of the exercise the purpose or objective of this activity, which may not immediately be clear or apparent [Also **the point** or **object of the exercise***]

- We're now going to see a short video. *The aim of the exercise* is to give a general explanation of how the product operates.
- *May I interrupt a moment ... ? You've been telling us about your company's plans without saying why; could you explain *the point of the exercise*?
- *So, to start with, I'm going to spell out *the object of this morning's exercise*, which is to look into ways of increasing productivity.

to arrange (for) to fix or make practical plans for something to happen or to be done

- Let's *arrange for* a meeting now. How about Friday, nine o'clock, your office?
- Well, everything seems to be agreed. Just one last thing before we draw up contracts; we need you to confirm that you can *arrange for* delivery of consignments within twenty-one days of order.
- OK, so we have *arranged for* finance and now we can go ahead with marketing.

game plan carefully thought out general strategy for achieving a target and the tactics and methods to be used

- The marketing *game plan* this year is to identify gaps in the market and to develop products specially designed to fill those gaps.
- The government's *game plan* for winning the election was clear from its manifesto.
- The *game plan* for this morning's meeting is to finish ordinary business in the first half hour, then take time out for coffee, so that, in the second half, we can zero in on the all-important question of new product development.

to go ahead to make progress; to move forward; to start or continue from a static or waiting position [Note: see examples for use as verb + preposition, phrasal verb, noun and adjective respectively]

- Local government has approved the plans for the new factory, so we can *go ahead* with construction.
- Now that you're leaving the company, you can *go ahead* and do what you want.
- The government has given the *go-ahead* to privatisation plans in the State sector of industry.
- This is a *go-ahead* company and we expect all staff to operate in line with this idea.

to go for (it) to be very enthusiastic and positive in feeling and action, usually about some specific thing or goal [informal]

- That's a good suggestion. In fact I could really *go for* that idea.

- Nothing in life is impossible. If you want it, *go for it.*
- Our new product gives us an advantage over our competitors in terms of both quality and cost. We need to get it on the market fast, so we can expand our market share. So, let's *go for it!*

in order to with the purpose or aim of doing or causing something; so as to

- A number of people visit our showroom simply *in order to* satisfy their curiosity, others are genuine customers.
- *In order to* demonstrate this theory, we carried out a number of experiments, with interesting results.

to make up one's mind to decide

- I haven't yet *made up my mind* whether to accept the offer or not.
- The chairman's *mind was made up*; he would offer to resign.

a means to an end way or method of getting to an objective

- A presentation may be only the first in a series of stages leading to some desired result. So, to that extent, it can be seen as *a means to an end.*
- We use special offers in order to attract bigger orders – in other words, as *a means to an end.*
- We have to reduce our overhead expenses. This will lead to job losses in some departments – an unpleasant fact, I'm afraid, but *the end justifies the means.*

on purpose not by accident or chance, but by or with some intention; deliberately

- Although the factory fire appeared accidental on the face of it, after a thorough investigation it became crystal clear to police and insurance claims investigators that it had been started *on purpose.*
- Although everyone has to be at the meeting on time, the chairman will be a few minutes late, as usual. He does this *on purpose*, just to let everyone know who's in charge.

to put together to assemble or fit together pieces or parts to make a whole

- We need to *put together* a flexible production plan to meet fluctuations in demand.
- At our North Carolina assembly plant, we *put together* the parts for our motors.
- Our competitors have the advantage over us in some areas and we have to *put together* an effective game plan to overcome this.
- The finance director has been offered a job with one of our competitors – we'll have to *put together* an alternative package and some strong arguments if we want her to stay.

to set up to establish; to found; to organise; to put in a position or condition to operate; to begin doing or making; to arrange [Note: *to set up* can be used as verb + preposition, phrasal verb or noun – see examples]

- The company *was set up* ten years ago.
- Is the equipment *set up* for the presentation?
- The government is to *set up* an investigation into the causes of last month's violent demonstrations.
- I'd like to show you a short video describing our company *set-up.*

to tackle to take firm direct and positive action in dealing with a threat or obstacle

- The government is doing all it can *to tackle* problems of housing and unemployment.

- 'The main generator's out of action and the emergency one's on the blink. Can you deal with it?'
  'Sure. We'll get an engineer over right away *to tackle* it.
- I can't help you with the wording of the contract – why don't you *tackle* the legal department about it?

to take action (on) to act, either in response to or as a result of circumstances, or some decision; to deal with

- We need *to take* firm *action*, now, *on* the reduction in our market share – before matters get worse.
- Changes in pricing policy and flexibility of product design; these are the two things we have to *take action on* above all.
- *We* cannot *take* any *action on* your proposals until you have dealt with the questions raised in our fax of 01 October, on which we await your reply.

to take steps to take a series of actions towards a specific objective

- As a rule, the company begins *taking steps* to recover unpaid accounts ten days after payment falls due.
- In the course of the next day or so, we *shall be taking steps* to put our plans into action.
- Yes, I agree we should *take steps* to reduce the workforce, but in any case we can't make any progress at all until the meeting with the unions has taken place.
- Although urgent *steps* have to *be taken* to protect our interests, we must take care not to cut corners; we have to make sure there are no mistakes.
- We cannot wait for our competitors to make a move before taking action; we have to *take* the necessary *steps* of our own accord.

to take the initiative to be the first to make a move, forcing others to react accordingly

- There's a gap in the market that we can fill – if we don't *take the initiative*, our competitors will, for sure.
- For this job, we're looking for someone with a go-ahead attitude, a self-starter, someone who's prepared to *take* and maintain *the initiative*.
- In making this offer, we *have taken the initiative* on behalf of our clients towards resolving the dispute. So now the ball is in your clients' court.

with a view to with the aim, purpose or object of (doing) something [Also **with an eye to***]

- We are opening an office in Budapest *with a view to* expansion in Eastern Europe.
- *Market analysts look into market trends *with an eye to* advising dealers on buying and selling shares and other securities.

Focusing

to come to the point to arrive directly at the focus, or most important part, of a speaking or writing activity

- I'm going *to come* straight *to the point*; the company is not satisfied with your performance – you're dismissed.
- I'm afraid I can't follow your reasoning; you've been speaking for twenty minutes without *coming to the point*.

the fact of the matter is (that) (emphatic) the truth is; the most important thing is

- You keep telling us that production is delayed because of equipment breakdown, when *the fact of the matter, as everyone knows, is that* the real reason is industrial action.
- Our products have been tested against similar products from other manufacturers. *The fact of the matter is that*, although some can compete with us on quality, none can compete in terms of price.
- As we have seen from the figures, *the fact of the matter is that*, although profits remain high, we have to replace dying products with new stars for the future.

to focus on to concentrate on; to direct one hundred per cent attention to

- Next, let's *focus on* production figures. As you can see from the graph, these have fluctuated over the last three months.
- The press *has* recently *focused* its attention *on* a number of financial scandals involving well-known public figures.

to get down to business to begin to talk seriously; to tackle the real or important matter(s)

- Right, if everybody is ready, let's *get down to business* at once. Then maybe we can finish the meeting in time for lunch.
- Now that terms have been agreed between us, we can leave it to the lawyers *to get down to* the serious *business* of drawing up the necessary documents.

to get to the bottom of to find the cause of, or the answer to, a problem or question

- Staff turnover is on the increase. Management are trying *to get to the bottom of* the matter.
- Our computer keeps on breaking down, so the engineers are checking it over to try and *get to the bottom of* it.

hard facts definite or specific facts which can be proved, checked or examined (in contrast to mere rumour, opinions, general statements or hopes) [Note: in the singular, this idiom is used to emphasise a single, usually unpleasant, fact]

- The survey produced a good deal of interesting information, but few *hard facts*.
- *The hard fact is* that we have a growing share of a shrinking market, and unless we diversify we'll go out of business for sure.

in contrast to (or **with**) different from; distinct from; opposite to

- *In* marked *contrast to* his usual relaxed, friendly manner, he appeared brisk and cold at the meeting.

- Sales figures have been on the increase over the past three months, *in contrast with* the same period last year, when they were falling.
- The results of Team A's research produced hard facts, *in contrast to* those of Team B, which had used hit and miss methods of data collection.

in fact the truth, or reality, is that; really; truly

- You've gone wrong in your calculations – you put the total at 650, when *in fact* it should be 648.
- According to what you said yesterday, you were prepared to go along with our proposals. What you're now saying, *in fact*, is that you've changed your mind.
- The machine looks difficult to operate but, *in fact*, it's dead easy – just push these two buttons and, hey presto! See, it's working!

in reality to be absolutely correct; really; actually

- Although in principle it would be possible to extract Antarctic minerals, it is not likely to happen *in reality*, at least, as long as the international protection treaty lasts.
- So, *in reality*, are you saying that you both agree and disagree with our proposal? I'm afraid you haven't made yourself clear.

in (this) respect focusing on only (one of) a number of factors; considering this factor in isolation

- The two successful companies differ *in this respect*: one is successful in its own right, as a manufacturer, and the other's success is due to its policy of acquisitions.
- We need to concentrate on our overseas markets; *in this respect* we are falling behind our competitors.
- The two products are similar *in some respects* but different *in others*.
- *In many respects*, this proposal looks interesting, although I have my doubts about some items.

- Now we are agreed *in all respects*, we can go ahead with the contract formalities.
- The letters are ready, except *in* just *one respect* – they need signing!

a matter of a factor likely to be influential; a situation, matter, issue, thing, question, problem or topic which is most important or on which something depends [Also **a question of***]

- The chairman confirmed that the cost-cutting operation had been a success and that it was just *a matter of* time before the company made a full recovery.
- Successful marketing is *a matter*, amongst other things, *of* identifying the right product for a particular market.
- *Whether or not we go ahead with the scheme is largely *a question of* raising the necessary finance.

to spotlight to put special focus or attention on (a person or thing) [Note: *spotlight* can also be used as a noun*]

- The finance department *has spotlighted* three areas where we are overspending; these need to be tackled as a matter of urgency.
- *As to staff performance this year, I'd like to put *the spotlight* on the sales manager for spare parts, who has done wonders.

to zero in on to identify and concentrate on some target

- Criminals are always quick *to zero in on* any new opportunity to make money; the fact that credit card fraud is no exception, perhaps proves the point.
- We need to come up with new products and *zero in on* new markets if we are to stay ahead of our competitors.
- As we're short of time, can we *zero* straight *in on* the question of production delays, which stand to damage our goodwill with customers if not tackled at once.

STUDY UNIT

8

Time

ahead of time (or **schedule**) earlier than arranged, expected or planned [Note: opposite in meaning to **behind time** (or **schedule**)*]

- As the meeting is running *ahead of time*, may I suggest we break off now for coffee, before we come to the main point on the agenda, instead of in thirty minutes' time as arranged.
- The Minister's arrival *ahead of schedule* caused a minor panic.
- Hello, I'm at my hotel. Yes, I'm early; my flight arrived *ahead of schedule*. Can we bring forward our meeting?
- *The meeting is running *behind schedule* and we have to finish on time, so we'll have to leave some items on the agenda until the next meeting.

at first originally; in the first instance; at/in the beginning; to start with; at the time of starting

- I thought he was joking *at first*, when he told me the police wanted to see me. The long and the short of it is, though, that I was arrested.
- It made sense *at first* to include overseas trade in our budget figures, but as time went on, we began to see that it needed to be treated separately.
- 'I'm sorry about the explosion at the factory. In future I'll make sure safety procedures are followed.' 'You should have thought of that at first.'

at once immediately; very soon; right away

- Would you come to my office. *At once*, please.

- Can you send this fax *at once* please, it's urgent.
- We need to leave *at once* if we're going to be in time for our flight.

as yet up to now; up to the time of speaking; so far

- We wrote to them a week ago but have not received a reply *as yet*.
- *As yet*, we have not had time to consider your proposals.
- This is a new process and we have not, *as yet*, completed safety tests.

at (or **from**) **the outset** at, from or shortly after some starting point; or from the first or early stages

- You were told *at the outset* – in fact, when you came here for interview – that smoking is not allowed in this office.
- *From the outset*, the machine had been difficult to operate and after several accidents, it was decided to modify and simplify the controls.
- The product was more successful than we had expected *at the outset*.

for the time being temporarily; for the moment

- We're ahead of our competitors *for the time being* but we can only stay that way as long as we keep an eye on what the market wants.
- That big customer still hasn't paid. That means we'll have to stall our own creditors *for the time being*, unless the bank lets us go further in the red.

in the course of during; while; while being done;

- The discussion moved back and forth *in the course of* the meeting.

- *In the course of* carrying out the tests, we came up against equipment breakdowns several times.
- Three men were injured while the tunnel was *in the course of* construction.

in future starting from this (or that) time; from now (or then) on

- You are late again and you haven't shaved. *In future* you should turn up on time, and shaved.
- So far, we have not had to face serious competition but *in future* this will not be the case.
- After a series of accidents at its factory, the company decided that *in future* proper action should be taken to ensure staff safety.

in the future at or during some future time

- I shall hope to see you again at some time *in the future*.
- *In the* foreseeable *future*, we are likely to have to replace much of our equipment.
- We foresee some interesting market developments *in the* near *future*.
- We are forging ahead with the marketing plan. It's taking rapid shape and *in the* fairly near *future* we plan to carry out dummy runs in selected areas before starting the main campaign.
- If the company continues spending money at the present rate, it'll be bankrupt *in the* not-so-distant *future*.

in the long run eventually; over or after a long time [Note: **in the short run** acts as a contrast to *in the long run**]

- *Hit and miss procedures may produce a few lucky successes *in the short run* but *in the long run* they are ineffective.
- We are ahead of our competitors at the moment, but we cannot maintain this position *in the long run* unless we improve our marketing.
- Sooner or later the recession will finish; everything comes to an end *in the long run*.

in the long (short or **medium) term** thinking, looking or planning from now into the future [Note: often used as an adjective*]

- This company offers advice on *short-term*, *medium-term* and *long-term* investment and financial planning in general.
- Regular maintenance of equipment provides immediate and *short-term* benefits. In a nutshell, it helps avoid unnecessary problems, but in itself offers no guarantee of trouble-free operation *in the long term*.

in the meantime meanwhile, for the time being

- We look forward to meeting you in Dublin on 3 April. *In the meantime*, please confirm flight number and estimated time of arrival so that we can arrange for you to be met at the airport.
- The new machines will not be installed for at least three months, so we must make do with the present ones *in the meantime*.
- I shall shortly be introducing you to our sales director but *in the meantime*, let me show you a short video in connection with company development.

in a moment shortly; very soon; almost immediately

- We don't have time for coffee – the meeting will be starting *in a moment*.
- I have some letters to sign, so if our visitors arrive, make them comfortable and tell them I'll be with them *in a moment*.

in time soon or early enough; not too late; at or before the right time

- The firefighters arrived just *in time* to prevent the blaze spreading to nearby buildings.
- The meeting starts at 1000. Please make sure you're here *in* good *time* so we can get down to business on time.

to look forward to to think about some future time or event with positive, good feelings

- Goodbye. I *look forward to* seeing you at next week's meeting.
- 'Perhaps you would like to come and visit us when next you're in Kyoto.' 'I'*ll look forward to* it.'

- This is a very difficult project. I must say I'm *looking forward* to finishing it.

moment of truth the final and unavoidable point of crisis, change, confrontation or decision

- He had been stealing money from the company for years and must have known that *the moment of truth* would come sooner or later.
- We're about to taste the first bottle from the 1983 vintage. This, ladies and gentlemen, is the *moment of truth*.
- The chairman, with his well-developed feel for timing, like a great sensualist trying to hold back *the moment of truth* indefinitely, delayed giving instructions for the takeover until the last moment.

on time exactly at the right time, not late

- Goods normally leave the factory *on time*. Any delays usually occur in the course of delivery.
- Please make sure delivery is *on time*, as we have a tight production schedule to keep to.

right (or **straight**) **away** now; immediately; at once

- This fax is urgent; could you send it *right away*, please?
- These losses are serious – we'll have to call a meeting *straight away* to get to the bottom of it.

so far up to now; as yet

- We need to make some changes in our pricing structure. *So far*, we haven't been allowing for some of our overheads and in future we have to make sure that we get it right.

- *So far* this year, we've allowed our competitors to take the initiative in overseas markets. We need to take immediate steps to tackle this, and in a moment I'll be explaining what I think we should be doing.
- 'How much money has been stolen from the company *so far*?'
  'Two million dollars in all, give or take a few cents.'

time out a pause or interval during some activity [Note: *time out* is often accompanied by verbs, 'to take' or 'to call'*]

- We don't seem to be making much headway in our discussion. Why don't we call *time out* for half an hour and then try again.
- *We're coming up against problems testing the equipment. We need to take *time out* to check our methods.

B

PRACTICE

The Marketing Game Plan

STORYLINE UPDATE

Boldmere PLC, a company specialising in electronic security systems, has provisionally patented a vehicle protection device called Auto Security Net (ASN). At a recent meeting, decisions were taken *as to* finance and marketing. These were summarised in a memo, with related graphics, from Jack Wagner (Chief Executive) to Norman Buchan (Finance Director) and Julia Van der Merwe (Marketing Director) (see page 12).

❶ WARM-UP

a. What sources of finance might a company *look into* when planning to market a new product?

b. *On the other hand*, what factors would a prospective lender *take into account* before coming to a decision?

❷ READING

The text below is an extract from a lecture to banking students. A banker is speaking about lending *in general*. You will see how the expressions in this book (mainly from Study Unit 1 in this case) can be used in a natural way to add polish and meaning.

As a rule, in the banking business, we like to say 'yes' to customers who come to us for credit. *For the most part*, they're just individuals or businesses trying to make an honest living, although there are *exceptions to the rule*, *of course*. And I'm glad to say that, in the main, we are able to help them.

We advise them to come to us with a proposal *on paper*, so we can look at it and see if we can accept it *in principle* – because the bank's policy is clear on the types of lending it can and can't do. We also *look into* the background of the customer. For example, we don't lend, *in general*, to people who have a bad credit record, and *in particular* to those with a history of changing banks – always a bad sign.

Anyway, if the customer's background is OK, we first look at the proposal *in theory* and then look at how it's likely to work *in practice*. And, *in the normal course*, we are able to help in some way. And, *on the whole*, our customers repay their loans, those who do not are *the exceptions that prove the rule*.

   The really bad customers? Well, as I said, we try to check people's credit history, so *nine times out of ten* we prevent these kind of people ('bad risks' we call them) becoming customers *in the first place*. I think the expression, 'prudence pays', *holds good* generally – and banking is certainly *no exception*.

❸ WRITING • SPEAKING PRACTICE

   a. Practise some of the idioms in Question 2 by writing a few sentences about an area of business you know about.

   b. Then make a short oral summary of what you have written, either to your partner, or onto a cassette if you are working alone.

❹ WORD STUDY

What is the meaning of the words and expressions below? They are used in Exercise 1 and 2 or in the letter, to First International Bank, in the Storyline. Show that you understand their meaning by using them in short sentences.

a. credit		**l.** fitted
b. glad		**m.** linked
c. to look at		**n.** transceiver
d. policy		**o.** sites
e. prudence pays		**p.** elements
f. a bad credit record		**q.** enable
g. sources		**r.** potential
h. factors		**s.** field trials
i. proposal		**t.** projection
j. combating		**u.** item
k. device		**v.** quoted

STORYLINE

In accordance with the decision taken at Boldmere's second planning meeting, Jack Wagner and Norman Buchan *put together* a brief written proposal for the company bankers, and submit it to them in the form of the following letter.

Boldmere plc

76 Blackstock Road
Finsbury Park
London N4 6QA
081 957 6929

26 January 19--

Mr D Evans
Assistant Manager
First International Bank Inc
73 Gracechurch Street
London EC3A 7UJ

Dear Mr Evans

Re: Proposal for medium-term finance: Auto Security Net (ASN)

Following our telephone conversation today, I confirm that my
company recently obtained a provisional patent (copy enclosed) for
our invention, which is aimed at combating auto thefts. In a
nutshell, ASN consists of an electronic device which can be fitted to
any vehicle. This in turn is linked to a network of transceiver
sites. In effect, these elements operate in conjunction to enable
tracing of stolen vehicles equipped with the device.

We believe there could be a wide market for this potential
breakthrough product. However, while the device in itself is
relatively cheap to produce, the major drawback is the likely high
cost of the system as a whole, arising from the need to set up the
transceiver site network. This could be worthwhile, depending on
market reaction.

In the circumstances, the company has decided to carry out field
trials, including site installation, on a limited scale, with a
view to testing the market but minimising the risk. However, in
order to do this, medium-term finance will be required.

Costing and cash-flow projections are enclosed. As you will see, we
are allowing for site installation as the major cost item, while on
the other hand unit price is quoted at the lowest estimate. We shall
of course be looking into ways of reducing the first and increasing
the second.

These are my company's proposals in bare outline. I look forward to
discussing them with you in detail on 7 February as arranged.

Yours sincerely

J. Wagner

J Wagner
Chief Executive

❺ WORD STUDY

In the left-hand column, below, are some expressions which you will hear in Question 6. Now look at the expressions on the right and try to find which is closest in meaning.

a. I hope it works for you	**1.** that looks acceptable in principle
b. that seems to be in order	**2.** tell me what you plan
c. if it comes to it	**3.** to make our actual expenses equal to our estimated
d. what do you have in mind?	**4.** good luck!
e. to tide us over	**5.** to meet our short-term needs
f. to meet our budget	**6.** the final reality is
g. the bottom line is	**7.** in that event(uality)

❻ LISTENING • NOTE-TAKING

 An Assistant Manager from First International, David Evans, is discussing Boldmere's financial proposals with Jack Wagner. Listen and take notes about:

- the two methods Boldmere will use to raise the finance
- the amount of money they want to borrow
- the form the loan will take
- the relationship Boldmere has with its parent company, Intersystems
- the time period of the loan

❼ WORD STUDY

What is the meaning of the words/expressions below which are often used in financial English? Some of them were used in the meeting you just listened to. Others can be found in the letter to Mr Wagner in the following storyline. Show that you understand their meaning by using them in short sentences.

a. to raise money	**h.** an overdraft	**o.** a facility
b. a borrowing	**i.** company statutes	**p.** second mortgage
c. shares	**j.** parent company	**q.** premises
d. bonds	**k.** a term	**r.** debenture
e. reserves	**l.** dead money	**s.** undertaking
f. substantial	**m.** security	
g. an issue	**n.** sound	

❽ TRANSFER

a. As David Evans, summarise Boldmere's proposal orally to your manager.

b. Now write the brief summary which your manager asks you to prepare so that the proposal can be *checked over in detail* before a decision is taken *as to* whether to approve it or not.

Shortly after his interview with the bank, Jack Wagner receives the following letter.

First International Bank Inc
73 Gracechurch St
London EC3A 7UJ
071 946 3821

Our Ref: AM/CR/9201

12 February 19--

Mr J Wagner
Boldmere plc
76 Blackstock Road
Finsbury Park
London N4 6QA

Dear Mr Wagner

Following our discussion on 7 February, the bank has now had an opportunity to examine your proposals.

On the whole, these appear sound and in principle the bank would be willing to provide a facility on the lines discussed. However, the security offered, that is to say, a second mortgage on the company premises, is not in itself sufficient to meet the bank's requirements, in view of the present state of the property market.

In the circumstances, the bank will require additional security in the shape of a debenture against the company's entire undertaking, in respect of the total facility.

If you will confirm on your company's behalf that this is in order, the necessary documentation can be drawn up ready for signature.

Yours sincerely

D. Evans

D. Evans
for *FIRST INTERNATIONAL BANK INC*

❾ TRANSFER

With regard to the security required by the bank, this is standard practice in the UK. What kind of security do banks look for in your own country?

⑩ WORD STUDY

In the left-hand column, below, are some expressions which you will hear in Question 12. Now look at the expressions on the right and try to find the one which is closest in meaning.

a. on the (marketing) side	**1.** please repeat
b. to go back to basics	**2.** to persuade
c. sounds good	**3.** very similar to
d. I didn't catch that	**4.** from the point of view (of marketing)
e. much the same as	**5.** focusing on fundamentals
f. to talk someone into (doing) something	**6.** I like that idea

STORYLINE

The Boldmere board *agreed to* accept the bank's terms. Once the necessary formalities had been dealt with, the board met to discuss marketing and development strategy. You will now hear Jack Wagner in discussion with Julia Van der Merwe and Narinder Dhillon, Boldmere's Technical Director.

⑪ WORD STUDY

What is the meaning of the words/expressions below, which are used in the storyline, in the meeting you are about to hear and in Question 14? Show that you understand their meaning by using them in short sentences.

a. terms	**g.** market	**l.** licence
b. formalities	**h.** trade	**m.** network
c. board	**i.** features	**n.** compatible
d. to fall within	**j.** benefits	**o.** facilities
e. to go public	**k.** approval	**p.** to access
f. company mission		

⑫ LISTENING • NOTE-TAKING • COMPREHENSION

a. Listen to the meeting and take notes about what Julia Van der Merwe and Narinder Dhillon are thinking about.

b. Make an oral/written summary of Julia Van der Merwe's views on the marketing line to be taken.

c. What statistics do you think she might *rely on in order* to promote ASN?

d. Make an oral/written summary of the two *points made* by Narinder Dhillon.

e. What do you think Julia Van der Merwe's idea, which she is beginning to form at the end of the recording, might be?

⓭ TRANSFER

How do you think ASN might best be developed and promoted?

⓮ READING

Read the following text of part of a lecture dealing with the *set-up* of British companies. Notice how the idioms from the Study Units in this book are used naturally to add polish and meaning.

> *For the most part*, British companies fall within the private sector. *In any case*, government policy *has brought about* a decrease in the number of state-owned companies as telecommunications, water, gas and electricity have *in turn* been through the privatisation programme.
>
> Companies in the private sector *consist of* two basic types, confusingly called 'public' and 'private'. Public companies *in general* are *large-scale* operations such as banks, insurance companies, and *of course* the privatised companies. However, public companies remain fewer in number than private companies which, *on the whole*, are smaller or family-run businesses.
>
> The difference between the two, *on paper at least*, can be found in their names. The word 'limited' (often shortened to 'Ltd') after a company name shows that it is private. *On the other hand*, the status of a public company is shown by the letters plc after its name. This is short for 'public limited company'. *In practice*, however, the real difference between the two *arises from* the fact that private companies cannot raise money by selling shares to the public, *in contrast to* public companies, which can do so by issuing shares and bonds to be offered *for sale* on the Stock Exchange. *In theory*, there is no reason why a private company cannot 'go public' but if it ever does come to it, *nine times out of ten* this is *to do with* growth, *in conjunction with* the need to raise a substantial amount of capital.

⓯ TRANSFER

Make an oral/written summary of company *set-up* in your own country.

Quantities

to amount to to total; to mean; to result in

- Current liabilities *amount to* $1.2m <u>in contrast with</u> liquid assets of $3.4m, so <u>the company</u> is in a strong position.
- Although <u>at first</u> the proposals seemed attractive, <u>in fact</u> *they amounted to* very little.
- This suggestion, if <u>carried out</u>, *would amount to* complete <u>disaster</u>.

and so on and other similar details; et cetera

- Last week, we discussed working conditions *and so on* in factories. Today, let's look at something completely different.
- I don't know him very well, although we've shared the same office *and so on* for two years.

as a whole taken or considered all together; <u>in aggregrate</u>

- The group *as a whole* approved the parent company's proposal.
- A general election is an opportunity for the people *as a whole* to voice their feelings about the government.

at all to any, or to some, extent or degree; in any way

- I'm not *at all* surprised that Stefan crashed his car; he drinks like a fish and drives like a lunatic.
- If we can be of any help to you *at all*, please do not hesitate to contact us.

at least to this minimum extent or amount or degree (and perhaps more)

- It's only a small order but *at least* it's better than nothing.
- I shall be in London for *at least* three days.

- Our objective this year is to gain *at least* a foothold for our products on the overseas market.
- No, £100 isn't enough; we need *at least* £150.

at (the) most up to (but certainly not more than) a given maximum

- Bankruptcy is certain; *at most*, we can just delay it, but we cannot prevent it.
- At £10 per unit, the price is too high. On an order of this size it should be £7 *at most*.
- I shall be in Tokyo for ten days *at the most*, certainly no longer.

at the outside as the highest estimate [Also means at the most]

- It takes twenty minutes *at the outside* from here to the station.
- 'How much does it cost?' '*At the outside*, I'd guess around £50.'
- Recovery from last year's losses will take a year <u>at least</u>, three years *at the outside*, <u>as long as</u> we maintain sales at the current rate.

to average out at to calculate or be calculated as an average

- Profits two years ago were £16m, last year £19m and this year £25m, which *averages out at* £20m a year over the period.
- Production time per unit *averages out at* two hours.

to be exact to be more precise; to define exactly or accurately

- As you may know, our company <u>made a</u> substantial <u>profit</u> last year – £15m, *to be exact*.

- We have about 300 employees – 286 *to be exact*.
- The calculations *were exact* to the nearest millimetre.

give or take more or less (by an approximate amount) than a certain amount [Note: *Give-or-take* can be used as an adjective*]

- The whole project is likely to cost about £1m, *give or take* a few thousand.
- *Give or take* an hour or so, we should be in Dresden in about twelve hours.
- *The salesman was only here for half an hour, so it's a very *give-or-take* estimate.

a good (or **great**) **deal of** much; a lot of (+ uncountable noun) [Note: **a good** or **great many** + countable noun has the same meaning*]

- Your training has cost the company *a good deal of* money.
- We have spent *a great deal of* time, energy and money on this project, so we are pleased to see it bearing fruit at last.
- *We've made *a good many* mistakes this year, and the biggest one was employing you.

in (the) aggregate when totalled; considered together (not individually); taken as a whole

- Individually, these losses are not in themselves very large, but *in the aggregate* they amount to a great deal of money.
- *In aggregate*, the advantages of moving our centre of operations outweigh the disadvantages.
- Looking at all aspects of the situation *in aggregate*, we can see that prospects are, on the whole, good.
- Synergy is the working of two or more forces or influences in conjunction to produce an effect which *in aggregate* is in excess of the total of their individual effects.

in all in total; altogether; all told

- Not many shareholders attended the meeting – only twelve *in all*.
- *In all*, we have about 300 regular customers.

- We have spent a great deal of money on this research project – some £2m *in all*.

in (or **of**) **all shapes and sizes** (being) of many or various different kinds, types, forms, measurements or descriptions

- Our shareholders are not only large companies; they are companies and individuals *of all shapes and sizes*.
- We have to decide whether we are selling our products to a limited, exclusive market, or to buyers *of all shapes and sizes*,
- In some countries, the range of cheeses and sausages is limited, whereas in others these products come *in all shapes and sizes*.

in excess of more than

- Company profits last year were *in excess of* £30m.
- Staffing levels are *in excess of* current requirements, so must be reduced.
- WEIGHT RESTRICTION: vehicles *in excess of* 10 tonnes laden weight may not cross this bridge.

in full completely; fully; totally; with nothing left out

- We insist on payment *in full* within seven days.
- As yet, I haven't read the report *in full*, though I've seen extracts.
- Once a month, the equipment must be checked over, *in full*.

more or less approximately; virtually; to a slightly bigger or smaller extent, amount or degree (than)

- One kilogram is *more or less* equivalent in weight to 2.2 English pounds.
- So, as we are *more or less* agreed in general terms, why don't we break off now and come back later to deal with each item in detail?
- 'Is the company merger successful?' '*More or less*, I think.'

on average taking an amount or figure which represents the combined total of a given number (x) of units divided by the total number of units (y)

- The highest monthly sales figures last year were £1.2m in July, the lowest were £0.5m in January, but *on average* they were £0.9m, taking the rest of the year into account.
- The working life of these machines is about two years *on average*.

on a (large) scale in (large) numbers; at a (high) level; to a(n) (great) extent. [Note: *small- (or large-) scale* can also be used as an adjective*]

- Production of the new model was limited at first, but it proved so popular that after a short time it was manufactured *on a large scale*.
- Although on the face of it the idea is a good one, we are not as yet prepared to invest money in it *on a large scale*.
- Our competitors are heavily involved in promoting their products in market sectors where we have held a dominant position. Commitment *on that scale* means that our market share is being seriously challenged.
- *The company is involved in *small-scale* production of high quality furniture.

or so approximately; about; roughly; more or less; give or take

- Only about ten people turned up at the shareholders' meeting, although thirty *or so* had been expected.
- 'How long does it take to drive from here to Frankfurt?' 'Usually an hour *or so*.'

10

STUDY UNIT

Position and Movement

back and forth movement from one position to another, before returning to the first position again, usually again and again, regularly [Also **backwards and forwards** and **to and fro***]

- Letters had been passing *back and forth* between the two companies for weeks before a meeting could be set up.
- *I've been travelling *to and fro* between Tokyo and Osaka for the past three months, so I'm glad to be staying here in Tokyo for a while.
- *I can see why the machine broke down – this part, here, should move freely, *backwards and forwards*, but look, it's jammed.

Every other (or **every second**) in a sequence, with the focus on the second, fourth, sixth and so on (or the first, third, fifth etc) [Also **every third**, **fourth**, **fifth** and so on*]

- We check equipment *every other* day, that is, three or four times a week.
- Quality control is carried out by testing *every other* unit.
- *Your company's products are very popular; it seems as if *every third* person in the country has one.

in lieu (of) instead (of)

- Normally, the company must give its employees one week's notice of dismissal. However, you are dismissed, effective immediately. Here is one week's pay *in lieu of* notice. Leave now.
- Employees travelling on company business can either stay at company-approved hotels at company expense, or they can claim reasonable accommodation expenses *in lieu* if they stay elsewhere.

- Your bonus is seven days' extra holiday or cash *in lieu*.

in place of instead of; as a replacement

- Factory production lines now often use robots *in place of* people.
- Credit cards are now widely used *in place of* cash or cheques.
- Our old computer is out-of-date; we should get a state-of-the-art one *in its place*.
- The shareholders removed the board of directors and appointed new directors *in their place*.

in turn in sequence; one after another; according to some pattern of events [Also means reciprocally*]

- The customs inspectors removed all the items from the suitcase and examined each one *in turn*.
- Thank you for your hospitality. *In turn*, we look forward to having you as our guest when you visit our country.
- *We are happy to provide the service you require. *In turn*, we would ask you to pay a small deposit and then monthly on account.

to vary from ... to (or **between**) to fluctuate between certain given limits [Also **to range from ... to***]

- Average sales *vary from* heavy in winter *to* light in summer.
- Staff attitudes towards company policy *vary between* neutral and ninety per cent positive.
- *Our prices *range from* £500 for a small unit *to* £5,000 for the top-of-the-range model.

Degrees of Difficulty and Probability

at will as or when one pleases; without restriction or limit

- Our showroom is open seven days a week, so that customers can come in any time and look around *at will*.
- With an Amex Gold Card, you can travel almost *at will*.
- Now that the government has lifted its import restrictions, our overseas competitors can operate in this country *at will*.

for sure this is certain; there is no doubt

- The economic crisis shows no sign of improving and we're deep in the red at the bank. If business improves and the bank extends our overdraft, we'll keep going, maybe. If not, we'll go bankrupt, *for sure*.
- 'The production department say they can produce 3,000 complete units a month.' 'Is that *for sure*? Last month they gave a different figure.'

in all probability most probably; more certain than not; in all likelihood

- *In all probability*, the new management team will bring about major changes in the company.
- According to informed sources, the recent loss of the government contract will *in all probability* have an impact on our share price.

in any case in any event; whatever happens; anyway

- I hope the meeting is over by 6 o'clock. *In any case*, I have to be at the airport in time to catch the 1930 flight.

- How you carry out the tests is up to you, but *in any case* don't cut corners; it's dangerous.
- I don't accept your argument about development costs but *in any case* it's beside the point as we don't have any funds for that purpose.

it's as simple as that the fact is so clear that no further reason or explanation is required

- We have two choices: either we increase the workforce or we don't meet the production deadline – *it's as simple as that*.
- Your argument is okay up to a point, but *it's not as simple as that*, there are some factors you've not allowed for.

no problem this is simple; without difficulty or inconvenience [informal]

- We can change the delivery schedules as you ask, *no problem*. But arranging for changes in specification at short notice, that's another matter, I'm afraid.
- If you're not prepared to do business on these terms, that's *no problem*; we have other customers interested.

of course this is natural or to be expected

- *Of course* the company is sympathetic with your personal problems, but if you cannot do your work you cannot expect to stay in your job, can you?
- Thank you for your letter, which has been passed to the Minister. I will, *of course*, let you know as soon as I have his response.

to rule out to forbid or prohibit the possibility; to consider as impossible

- Last year's poor trading performance *does not* necessarily *rule out* our expansion programme.
- Further contract negotiations *were ruled out* when the other side announced that they had awarded the contract to another company.
- The new law effectively *rules out* imports of cars, by imposing an impossibly high import duty on them.

a safe bet almost one hundred percent certain [informal]

- If you want a good lawyer, mine's *a safe bet* – she gets to the bottom of a problem, gives realistic advice and doesn't let you waste money on a dead-end case.
- 'Our sales in South America are down, although our customer relations are excellent. So, why?'
  'In my view, it's *a safe bet* that our competitors have been active without our knowledge.'
- As to the travel arrangements for your trip, although a car is convenient, there could be problems on the roads; your *safest bet* would be to go by train.

to stand to to be in a position where, if and when an event takes place, some advantage or disadvantage is likely to occur [Also **to stand a chance***]

- This year's bad weather has hit some crops so badly that prices *stand to* rise on the commodity markets.
- This invention gives us an advantage over our competitors and we *stand to* profit by it, as long as we use it in the best way.
- *By investing carefully, we *stand a chance* of making a profit.
- A takeover by our competitors? They don't *stand a chance*!

to take place to happen; to occur

- In the normal course, company sales meetings *take place* every other Friday at our Frankfurt office, starting at 1400.
- What *took place* during the meeting between the two presidents proved to be the first step towards a joint venture.
- A short-term decrease in interest rates is expected *to take place* as a result of steps taken by the government.
- In view of the urgency, discussions, which had been delayed, *will* now *take place* at once.

12
STUDY UNIT

Effective Methods

to allow for to take into consideration or account
- Estimates of delivery time abroad should *allow for* customs clearance.
- Working time lost through sickness and other causes must *be allowed for* when calculating the time required for a particular job.
- Company cash-flow projections are inaccurate: they do not *allow for* bad debts or salary increases.

better safe than sorry it is better to be too careful than to take risks
- Everyone must wear a safety helmet when visiting the construction site – *better* to be *safe than sorry*.
- Every stage of the process is checked three times, on the basis that it's *better* to be *safe than sorry*.
- Drivers are warned that road conditions could be dangerous so, if your journey isn't really necessary, stay at home; *better safe than sorry*.

bit by bit in small pieces or stages; gradually [Note: *Bit-by-bit* could possibly be used as an adjective*]
- At first, you may find the process as a whole difficult to understand; but if you examine it *bit by bit* you'll see it's not really so complex.
- Although the sales target seems a long way off at the moment, we seem to be getting there *bit by bit*.
- *I know it seems like a *bit-by-bit* process at first sight, but when you understand the procedure fully, you will see how each step fits together in a smooth progression.

to carry out to fulfil; to perform; to complete or finish successfully
- The oil company is *carrying out* geological surveys in the area before drilling begins.
- Since you have failed *to carry out* your agreement to repay the loan and interest by the due date, we are taking steps to recover by legal process.

to check over to look at carefully and efficiently in order to find out if there are any problems or mistakes [Note: *checkover* can be used as a noun* and as an adjective – see Unit 13 for 'hit-and-miss' checkover procedures']
- Letters should *be checked over* for mistakes before being sent.
- *Airline ground crews give all aircraft a *checkover* before takeoff.

a dry (or **dummy**) **run** an experiment or trial of a machine or project under realistic (but not real) conditions
- Before launching a national market survey, the market researchers carried out several *dry runs* at local level in order to test the reaction to their questionnaire.
- Before making a presentation, it's a good idea to do *a dummy run* by recording yourself on video or cassette and checking the result.

in depth completely and in detail; not superficially [Note: *in-depth* can be used as an adjective*]
- At first sight, these proposals seem interesting but we need to study them *in depth* before reaching a conclusion.

38

- At our last meeting, we discussed the subject in bare outline. We now need to examine it bit by bit, *in depth*.
- *An *in-depth* analysis of the test results produced some surprising conclusions.

in detail with every part, detail or item mentioned or included

- The machine should be checked over *in detail* once a month.
- Having seen the process in bare outline, let's now look at it *in detail*.
- Your report must be *in detail*, based on hard facts – nothing hit and miss – and should be delivered in ten days at the outside.

the ins and outs (of) all the details

- First of all, I want to present a bare outline of the situation; we'll go into *the ins and outs* of it later.
- You have the information. The facts speak clearly for themselves, so I really don't think it necessary to discuss all *the ins and outs*.
- Our brochure explains *the ins and outs* of how to operate the equipment.

to keep an eye on to watch carefully; to guard, in case of some (stated or unstated) risk or possibility

- The company employs security guards to *keep an eye on* our offices.
- We *keep a* careful *eye on* share price movements in market sectors where we do business.
- While the Minister is away, his deputy will *be keeping an eye on* things.

to look into to investigate; to examine carefully; to inquire

- There's a problem with the photocopier – can you send one of your engineers *to look into* it?
- Following the collapse last week of a major investment company, police are *looking into* its affairs.
- We need more information about the government's fiscal intentions next year. We'd better get our political contacts *to look into it*, discreetly of course.

to make sure (or **certain**) to ensure; to check or verify [Also means to cause or make something inevitable*]

- Hallo, caller, I think the person you want is out of the office at the moment but *I'll* just *make sure*. Can you hold?
- When you check over the equipment, *make* absolutely *sure* that all components are in good working order.
- I'll see you on Tuesday, then; and don't forget, *make sure* you bring the papers with you.
- *The loss of the government contract *makes* some redundancies almost *certain*.

to plan (or **think**) **ahead** to prepare for the future; to make calculated future arrangements

- The purpose of this meeting is *to plan ahead* for next year's marketing strategy.
- If *you had planned ahead*, you could have avoided some of the problems you came up against.
- If we're going to stay ahead of our competitors, we need *to think ahead*.

to take care (**not**) (**to**) to make sure/certain of (not) doing something

- When using this machine, *take care* to operate it in accordance with the instructions. If you don't, it will go dead on you.
- If we *don't take care* to provide an efficient after-sales and spare parts service for our customers, in the long run they will buy products from our competitors.

- In view of the bad road conditions, drivers are advised *to take care not* to drive in excess of 50kph.
- An insurance actuary must *take care* to be exact when calculating premiums, allowing for all possibilities and taking all necessary factors into account.

to think out to plan or consider carefully, in depth, in every aspect, especially something to be decided now which may be of future importance

- There's no easy solution to this problem, it has to *be thought out* carefully.

- The main purpose of this meeting is *to think out* our marketing strategy.

to try out to test or use (something or someone) for a trial period [Note: *try-out* can also be used as a noun*]

- We should *try out* the new equipment on a limited scale before going into production.
- *If you come to work for us, we'll give you a *try-out* in different departments at first, to see if you like us and we like you.

C

PRACTICE

A Technical Demonstration

STORYLINE UPDATE

Boldmere PLC, corporate specialists in electronic security systems, have obtained a provisional patent on a vehicle anti-theft device called Auto Security Net (ASN). Decisions taken *with regard to* finance and marketing are summarised in a memo with related graphics on page 12. Proposals for *short-term* finance for Boldmere's limited initial objectives (see letter page 29) have been agreed with the company bankers.

The Boldmere board – Jack Wagner (Chief Executive), Julia Van der Merwe (Marketing Director), Norman Buchan (Finance Director) and Narinder Dhillon (Technical Director) – met a few days ago to discuss marketing and development strategy. One important question was whether ASN was compatible with an existing telecommunications system operated by Saturn.

STORYLINE

Discreet *in-depth* enquiries *carried out* by Narinder Dhillon established that ASN was compatible with the Saturn system. *In the meantime*, Julia Van der Merwe developed an outline marketing strategy. The Boldmere team finally *thrashed out* the *game plan* summarised in the following memo.

Boldmere plc

From: JW

To: JM/NB/ND

Auto Security Net: development and marketing: strategy and tactics

In bare outline, our overall game plan is twofold:

- **Development** to obtain official licence(s) and practical facilities to operate the system, in the Greater London area at first, but with a view to wider-scale activities in the future.
- **Marketing** to make the market aware of the need for ASN and in addition offer some inducement in order to soften them up.

As to **development**, in the first place we need the police to go along with the idea, as we shall be working hand in hand with them; also as a means to an end – in order to add weight to our application for a DTI code operator's licence. In addition, police back-up will be useful on the marketing side (see below). So to start with, we need to open doors with the police by arranging for a technical demonstration. In the meantime we look into DTI requirements in detail to make sure we stand a good chance of obtaining the licence. ND to take the necessary action in this area, keeping JW in touch with developments. In the second place, we break the ice with Saturn and look into the possibility of tying ASN in with their existing Greater London network and, in the short term, doing a dry run using their facilities. JW to take steps here.

With regard to **marketing**, first and foremost we need up-to-date statistics on UK vehicle theft and recovery rates, Greater London traffic volume, consumer product attitudes, existing market product type and mix, motor theft insurance claims, motor insurance premium rates. Here we are aiming at illustrating market need for ASN. Results of this first step will determine the exact line we take on marketing. One angle already decided is to establish our credibility with motor insurers with a view to persuading them to reduce premiums for vehicles fitted with ASN. The fact that the success of the system depends on police cooperation may help to prove our case with the insurers – and in turn with the market – and on that basis motor insurers will be invited to technical demos, where the simple fact of a police presence could have the necessary impact. Once we have reached first base with the police and the motor insurers, we can then approach the market (motor manufacturers and accessory dealers) with a package. Only when the system is in operation in Greater London can we look into wider marketing opportunities. JM to tackle this area, in conjunction with ND on the technical side and keeping JW in the picture.

JW to coordinate and keep an eye on developments generally.

J

❶ WARM-UP

What factors need *to be taken into account* before making a technical demonstration? You will find some suggestions in the Answer Key.

❷ WORD STUDY

In the left-hand column, below, are some expressions used in the game plan and storyline. Now look at the expressions on the right and try to find the one that is closest in meaning.

a. discreet
b. to establish
c. outline
d. twofold
e. inducement
f. application
g. back-up
h. to illustrate
i. to determine
j. angle

1. summary, showing important factors
2. persuasion or incentive
3. support or help
4. to have a decisive influence on
5. point of view or method of approach
6. careful, tactful, secret
7. formal request
8. to show or prove to be true
9. consisting of two parts
10. to make clear or explain by using examples

STORYLINE

In accordance with the *game plan*, an initial approach was made to the DTI, the police, motor insurers and Saturn. Information on traffic volumes, car thefts *and so on* were readily available and within a few weeks a series of technical demonstrations was *taking place* in the Greater London area; the audiences being from major motor insurers and the police. In Question 5 you are going to hear Narinder Dhillon, Boldmere's Technical Director, speaking to one such audience. Among the audience are Joe Davis, from the Thames Valley Police and Evelyn George, attending *on behalf of* a leading motor insurer. But first, have a look at the graphics distributed to the audience beforehand.

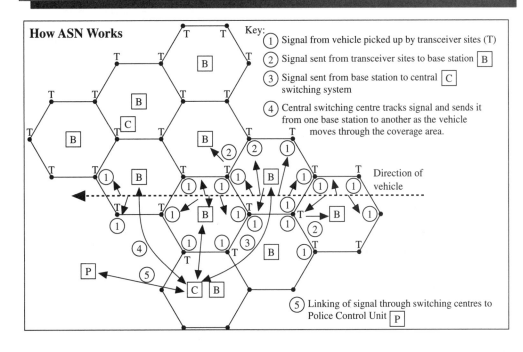

How ASN Works

Key:
1. Signal from vehicle picked up by transceiver sites (T)
2. Signal sent from transceiver sites to base station [B]
3. Signal sent from base station to central [C] switching system
4. Central switching centre tracks signal and sends it from one base station to another as the vehicle moves through the coverage area.

Direction of vehicle

5. Linking of signal through switching centres to Police Control Unit [P]

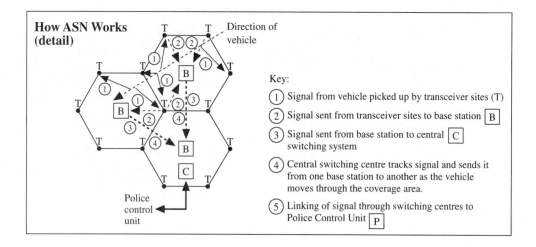

❸ DICTIONARY REFERENCE

In the demonstration you will hear the following expressions *in connection with* vehicles, electronics and crime. *In case* you do not know their meaning, check in a good dictionary. You may need to refer to a specialised dictionary.

Vehicles: alternator   generator   make (noun)   model (noun)   registration mark

Electronics: power source   computer generated and controlled   cells   digital   analogue

Crime prevention: auto theft prevention   burglar alarm   car alarm   anti-theft device   arrest and conviction rates

❹ WORD STUDY

Before listening to the first of the four parts of the demonstration, complete the blanks in Part 1 using the idioms in the box below, all of which appear in the Study Units.

the long and the short of it is   get down to business   on behalf of it's as simple as that   in particular   the aim of the exercise is straight away   the facts will speak for themselves   a breakthrough in our opinion

Part 1

Narinder Dhillon: (a) _____ _____ _____ my company, I'd like to

welcome you to this demonstration. (b) _____ _____, may I thank you for

your time, which I know is valuable to you, so I propose to (c) _____

_____ _____ _____ (d) _____ _____. (e) _____ _____

_____ _____ _____ _____ to demonstrate a new product developed and patented by my company. We call this product Auto Security Net, or ASN for short, and (f) _____ _____ _____ _____ _____ _____ _____ _____ that this product, (g) _____ _____ _____, is (h) _____ _____ in auto theft prevention, (i) _____ _____ _____ _____ _____. But we are confident that (j) _____ _____ _____ _____ _____ _____.

❺ LISTENING

 Now listen to Part 1 of the demonstration and check your answers to Question 4.

❻ WORD STUDY

The idioms and expressions in the left-hand column, below, appear in the tapescript of the technical demonstration, but not in the Study Units. Try to find their meaning by matching them with the expressions on the right. Then make sentences using these expressions.

a. for short	**1.** event
b. to locate	**2.** fault/something missing or not working
c. payout	**3.** to act on or together in close relation
d. incident	**4.** approximately
e. vulnerable	**5.** as an abbreviation
f. defect	**6.** not being used enough or at all
g. lack of use	**7.** state/condition of being too full
h. picked up	**8.** at a level of
i. interact with	**9.** to discover the position of
j roughly	**10.** to give help or support
k. overcrowding	**11.** result
l. to handle	**12.** payment of claim
m. outcome	**13.** to operate, control, manage or deal with
n. running at	**14.** detected or received
o. to back up	**15.** easily open to

❼ LISTENING • NOTE-TAKING • COMPREHENSION

   a. Listen to Part 2 of the demonstration and take notes about the consequences of car theft.
   b. The simulated theft of Narinder Dhillon's car was done *on purpose*. Why?
   c. What does Dhillon mean by 'special hotels'?

❽ WORD STUDY

Before listening to the third part of the demonstration on cassette, complete the blanks in Part 3 of the tapescript using the idioms in the box below, all of which appear in the Study Units.

more or less	to spotlight	by the way	consists of	at all
paying the penalty	that is to say	triggers off	rely on	in effect
to do with	allowing for	in brief	in turn	in all

Part 3

Dhillon: ASN (a) _____ _____ an electronic device fitted to the alternator, or generator as some people call it, and this (b) _____ _____ is powered by the engine so it doesn't have to (c) _____ _____ stored power or a power source vulnerable to defect or lack of use, such as a battery. This device (d) _____ _____ a signal when the engine is running. There are two important factors (e) _____ _____ about this signal. First, each signal has its own unique digital code. This is (f) _____ _____ _____ the make, model, colour and registration mark of the vehicle. Second, the signal itself is digital, (g) _____ _____ _____ _____ it is computer-controlled, computer-generated and interpreted, when necessary, thus (h) _____ _____ greatly increased capacity within the system at any given time.

Anyway, when transmitting, the signal covers a radius of one kilometre (i) _____ _____ _____ and is picked up by one or more of a network of transceiver sites already in place and arranged as a network of cells. Each cell interacts with its neighbour (j) _____ _____ _____ and (k) _____ _____ the entire network is coordinated by a series of roughly ten switch centres (l) _____ _____ which cover the whole of the Greater London area. As I said, the signal is only interpreted (m) _____ _____ when needed, (n) _____ _____, when the vehicle is stolen. The police will have access to the switch centres. So, all I have to do is call the police, the police then access the switch centre and this indicates the position of the vehicle to within a thousand square metres. (o) _____ _____ _____, this is a silent signal, so the thief has no idea that he will soon be (p) _____ _____ _____ for his actions.

9 LISTENING

 Now listen to Part 3 of the demonstration and check your answers to Question 8.

10 LISTENING • NOTE-TAKING • COMPREHENSION

 a. Listen to Part 4 of the demonstration and take notes on the questions asked and the answers given.

b. What expression does Dhillon use to change topics?

c. Why is a digital system used in preference to analogue?

d. How does PCN operate?

e. Does Boldmere need to get a full DTI code operator's licence now?

f. Does Dhillon say that ASN is to operate in Greater London only?

g. Why is ASN being promoted when there are other devices on the market?

11 TRANSFER • WRITING

Imagine you are Joe Davis, from the Thames Valley Police, who attended the demonstration. Write a report summarising the important points from the technical demonstration. Refer to the graphics.

12 TRANSFER • SPEAKING

Describe some process you are familiar with, preparing your own graphics and referring to them during your presentation/demonstration.

13
STUDY UNIT

Ineffective Methods

(at) random without specific aim; unsystematic [Note: *random* can also be used as an adjective*]

- In a lottery, winning numbers are drawn *at random*.
- *The company's policy of sending *random* mailshots was not cost-effective.
- The market researchers interviewed people *at random* in the street.

(by) trial and error finding the right method or solution by the primitive process of making changes in measurements or calculations until finally there are no errors [Note: *trial-and-error* can also be used as an adjective*]

- *This is a dangerous chemical. Tests on it must be carefully thought out in advance; simple *trial-and-error* testing could prove fatal.
- After a good deal of *trial and error*, we found the exact proportions required for the mixture.
- The company doesn't have money to waste on testing *by trial and error* – you must be more systematic in your approach.
- He had forgotten the formula for producing the result he wanted, but he arrived at the answer through a process of *trial and error*.

to cut corners to follow a quick but risky route to an objective, especially by not performing all the usual stages of some process

- In this company we don't *cut corners*; we produce a high-quality, reliable product.
- He's a brilliant research chemist, but *he cuts* too many *corners*. One day he'll blow us all up.

hit and miss unsystematic; random; relying on chance; not properly thought out or carried out

- The experiment went wrong because of *hit-and-miss* methods.
- Your proposition is based partly on fact and partly on imagination – in other words, it's rather *hit and miss*.
- The machine must be carefully checked over before use, then it will work. You'll find that most cases of breakdown stem from *hit-and-miss* checkover procedures.

the line (or **path**) **of least resistance** the easiest (though probably not the best) way or course of action [Same as to take the easy way out]

- The company collapse was brought about by managers *taking the line of least resistance* in the face of mounting problems.
- For several years, the company has been taking *the path of least resistance*; in a nutshell, relying on sales of successful products to existing customers.

(a) short cut a quicker way or method than usual of reaching an objective, by not following the usual way, pattern or procedure

- On the whole, there are few *short cuts* to making money. Many *short cuts* lead to dead ends.
- In some countries, the quickest *short cut* through trading problems resulting from government regulations can be by making secret payments to key government personnel. This can be a legitimate means to an end, while other cultures view it as corruption.
- Although the end product is excellent, the process needed to achieve it is too complex and expensive. Are there no *short cuts*?

(a) soft option an easier, less inconvenient (and generally less effective) method or course of action than others available or possible

- As a rule, *soft options* do not pay dividends in the long run.
- Action taken by the government in respect of unemployment has amounted to nothing more than a series of *soft options*: too little, too late and all in vain.

to take (a) chance(s) (on) to try to do, or to take action on something, knowing that there is a possibility of negative results; to run (a) risk(s)

- We've taken advice on our problem but we still can't make our minds up about the right action to take. We really don't want to *take* any *chances* so we've decided to get a second opinion.

- In theory, we, as an investment company, offer our clients 'maximum security' for their money; while in practice – and strictly off the record – we *take chances* with their money as a matter of course.
- With hindsight, it seems clear that the company's problems arose from the managers' *taking* too many *chances*. But it's easy to be wise after the event.

to take the easy way out (of) to avoid dealing directly with a problem, difficulty or situation by taking some other action [Same as to take the line of least resistance]

- The executive tried *to take the easy way out of* his family problems through alcohol, which only made matters worse.
- We've got a real problem. There's *no easy way out*, I'm afraid; we've just got to face up to it.
- In view of his terrible problems, which could involve bankruptcy, even imprisonment, he considered going abroad – even committing suicide – but decided that in both cases that would be *taking the easy way out*.

to take risks or **to run the risk of** to follow a course of action, knowing that it may lead to negative results; to take (a) chance(s)

- I don't want to *run the risk of* being impolite, but you have been speaking for ten minutes and I'm still totally in the dark. So would you please make it clear what you're aiming at.
- In these negotiations, if we don't find some common ground early on, we *run the risk of* reaching a stalemate.

14

STUDY UNIT

Progress

all systems go to be in a condition or attitude of total readiness to go ahead [informal]

- We've set up the game plan, now it's *all systems go*.
- 'How do you feel about the new project?' 'I'm on *all systems go*.'
- Right, let's see if this machine works. Push this button here, turn that switch there. What's gone wrong? It should be *all systems go*.

to break new ground to enter a new area of discovery or knowledge; to be a pioneer

- This exciting development in electronics *breaks new ground* and offers many interesting possibilities.
- The recent agreement between the company and the unions *has broken new ground* in industrial relations.
- So far, our researchers have covered only familiar territory; now, we're about to *break new ground*.
- I don't believe this product has been marketed as widely as possible. I'm sure there's *new ground to be broken*.

to break the ice to do or say something to ease tensions between people; to start to create a more sociable, relaxed atmosphere, usually on first meeting [Note: *icebreaking* could be used as a noun* or as an adjective – as in an *icebreaking* meeting]

- Sales technique is the art of *breaking the ice* between supplier and consumer.
- A new manager's first task is *to break the ice* with staff and create a new team dynamic.
- Your presentation was not bad, but not as successful as it could have been. You never really *broke the ice*.

- *Look, this is going to be a tough negotiation. I suggest taking time out for *icebreaking* before we start.

to break through to make sudden, positive progress by pushing through a seen or unseen barrier or obstacle [Note: *breakthrough* can be used as a noun*]

- *The discovery of the petrol engine was *a breakthrough* in the history of transport.
- After months of patient negotiation, the company finally *broke through* the wall of official regulations and was able to do business with the government.

to come up with to create; devise; produce; find

- During this century, scientists *have come up with* many practical ideas to improve the quality of life. Nature, on the other hand, amuses herself with her own game plan.
- This artwork is rubbish! Can't you *come up with* anything better than that?

- Our creditors are <u>putting the pressure on</u> – we'll have to *come up with* at least a <u>short-term</u> answer <u>right away</u>.

to forge ahead to make very good or rapid progress against all resistance; to develop or improve quickly

- We're *forging ahead* with the construction scheme; the first two stages were completed <u>ahead of schedule</u>.
- After last year's poor results, the company *is forging ahead* towards recovery.
- The project, which was little more than an idea a year ago, *has forged ahead* since then.

to get to (or **to reach**) **first base (with)** to complete <u>the first step</u> of a series of stages towards some objective [Note: possible variation, **to get past/beyond first base**, appears in Practice Section B Exercise 6 in the recorded material – see the tapescript in Answer Key]

- We've <u>arranged for</u> our share of the finance for the project, but if our partners don't <u>come up with</u> their share, the whole <u>thing's</u> going to <u>go dead</u> before we *get to first base*.
- OK, we've <u>broken the ice</u> with these people, who could become big customers. They've agreed to listen to our proposals. A meeting <u>has been set up</u> for next week and we have to make a really effective presentation of our products and services to <u>stand any chance</u> of *getting to first base* with them.

to make headway to make <u>progress</u> in a particular direction, in spite of any problems or difficulties

- The engineers *are making* some *headway* with the repairs, although it will be several days before the work is finished.
- I don't seem *to be making* much *headway* in my career.
- Some *headway has been made* in cutting costs – about $50k <u>so far</u> this year.
- We're *making* reasonable *headway* in the negotiations, but we've a long way to go <u>as yet</u>.

to make progress to move forward; to advance or to improve from some actual or imaginary starting point towards some actual or abstract objective

- We *made* slow *progress* driving through the city because of heavy traffic.
- The engineers *have made* excellent *progress* installing the new equipment and they are three days <u>ahead of time</u>.
- <u>As yet</u>, we have *made* little *progress* in our negotiations.
- She *has made* remarkable *progress* since joining the company. Five years ago she was a secretary, now she's systems manager.

to open doors (for) to prepare the ground for some future development; to create possibilities or opportunities; to <u>break through</u> obstacles [Also **to pave the way (for)***]

- The chairman's assistant is an effective operator in public relations. She *has opened doors for* the company with many new and potential customers.
- Many ideas and philosophies <u>aimed at</u> *opening doors for* humanity <u>go wrong</u> in the hands of fanatics, opportunists and inadequates, when they <u>take shape</u> as narrow ideologies based <u>on value judgements</u>. <u>That is</u>, they acquire the '-ism' <u>suffix and</u>, <u>by the same token</u> produce a <u>dud end product</u>.
- *The recent agreement between our two companies *has paved the way for* future cooperation between us.

(a) step (forward) positive movement towards an objective or improvement

- The recent agreement between the company and the unions <u>amounts to</u> *an* important *step forward* in industrial relations.
- Yesterday, discussions between the two companies took *a step forward* when they agreed, <u>in essence</u>, not to <u>insist on</u> settlement of their claims <u>in full</u>.
- Seen <u>in the light</u> of its past performance, the government's present policy on training for the unemployed is *a* definite *step in the right direction*.

- Although in the aggregate we find your proposals unacceptable, they are at least *a step towards* smoothing out some of the problems which have arisen.

to take shape to progress from some general or uncertain theory, idea or plan towards something with definite shape or form (but not yet completed)

- This construction project is on a very large scale. To begin with, we faced a good many problems and drawbacks, and a lot of things went wrong. However, we coped with all of these and it's now beginning *to take shape*.
- Plans for the new car *are taking shape*, although the finished product will not be exactly on the lines of the original design.

- By the end of the meeting, ideas for marketing the new product had begun *to take shape*.

to take (a) step to take some particular action

- Before signing the contract, we should *take the step* of consulting our lawyers.
- 'I've decided to fire your secretary.' 'Oh, really? I'm rather taken aback that you should *take a step* like that without discussing it with me first. I might not agree to it.'
- I'd argue against *taking* such *a step* as the finance director suggests, on the grounds that it's too risky – and we can't afford to take chances with shareholders' money.

15

STUDY UNIT

Problems and Solutions

all or nothing to be or to be aiming at one hundred per cent of something, the only alternative being zero per cent. [Note: *all-or-nothing* can be used as an adjective*]

- *This company has an *all-or-nothing* policy with its smaller suppliers; we guarantee orders and buy their total production, while they supply no-one else. That way, we control prices.

- The housing market was static for months, then, with the improvement in capital markets, it became so active that it was almost impossible to cope with. It seems it's a matter of *all or nothing*.

back against the wall in a very difficult position; with few or no choices as to what action to take

- The minister had survived many political changes, many threats to his position. In fact, when he had his *back against the wall*, he was at his most charming, and his most dangerous.

- OK, so we didn't even get to first base with that potential customer, but our *back's not against the wall* yet. We have to think over our game plan again.

to compete against to try to beat or to oppose in competition

- Recent increases in taxation mean that companies are *competing* as much *against* the government as *against* each other.

- In this company, our policy is to work as a team: if *we're competing against* each other, we can't *compete* successfully *against* our rivals in business.

to cope (with) to manage a problem; to deal successfully with a difficulty

- The new product was so successful that production was barely able *to cope with* demand.

- Unless our budget is increased, the department simply *cannot cope* any longer.

- We have enough problems already, and now there are staff shortages *to cope with*.

to cut one's losses to end or withdraw from a bad situation which can only get worse [Note: *loss-cutting* could be used as an adjective as in a *loss-cutting* operation]

- This product has almost outlived its lifespan – we should *cut our losses* and take it off the market at once.

- Reliable sources inform us that the bank's second half results will disclose further losses and write-offs of bad debts. As your investment brokers, we have to advise you to consider *cutting your losses* and selling your shares now, against holding out for an upturn in the future.

(a) drawback a disadvantage

- Your suggestion has only one serious *drawback*; that is, it's likely to reduce profit margins.

- That seems an excellent idea. I can't see any *drawbacks*.

to face up to to accept something difficult or unpleasant and confront it

- Retirement is something we all have to *face up to* sooner or later.
- The company has serious problems, which must *be faced up to* and dealt with if we are to survive.

in the (or **as a**) **last resort** the only real or remaining answer or possibility when every factor or possibility has been examined, considered or tried

- If the marketing manager's poor performance continues, then *in the last resort* the company will have to remove him and replace him with someone else.
- We have to look into ways of reducing expenditure. As unemployment is already high, then dismissal of staff should only be considered *as a last resort*.

(a) long shot an attempt which is unlikely to succeed

- These proposals for marketing ice cream in Greenland seem rather *a long shot*.
- The research and development department have come up with a new idea. They say it's *a long shot*, but worth trying. We have to decide whether it's worth risking the money.
- If you can't book a flight, try and get a standby ticket at the airport – it's *a long shot*, but you might be lucky.
- In principle, I like the idea, but I'm afraid *it's* just *too long a shot* in the present market.

to make do (with) to manage with or accept something which is less than one wants or needs, because there is no other choice

- We can't afford new cars for executives until next year, so they'll have to *make do with* their present ones in the meantime.
- The government has made it clear to defence chiefs that no extra money will be made available this year and that they will just have to *make do*.

- I'm afraid we simply *can't make do* any longer *with* this old equipment – we'll have to replace it.
- They're obviously not prepared to up their offer so, are we going to *make do with* what we can get, or try elsewhere?

make or break to be the cause or instrument of success or failure [Note: examples show normal use as adjective or verb]

- Be very careful how you treat the chairman's wife, she has a great influence over her husband. In effect, she can *make or break* a young executive like you.
- Negotiations broke down last week but both sides are coming together again today in a *make or break* effort to find common ground on which to base further discussions.

on the blink not working properly; needing servicing or repair [informal]

- I'm afraid there'll be a delay clearing these cheques through your account; our head office computer is *on the blink*.
- No, I didn't get the message; our lines of communication must be *on the blink*.

to run (or **come** or **be**) **up against** to be, or arrive, at a position where positive progress or forward movement is, or may be, blocked

- The researchers *came up against* a problem when actual tests gave a different result from that predicted in the circuit diagram.
- Profits have fallen because the company *is up against* stronger competition than expected.
- The government *ran up against* strong opposition when it tried to increase taxes.

to save the situation to find an answer to a serious problem [Also **to save the day***] [Note also **to save** (or **lose**) **face** meaning to save (or lose) dignity, reputation or honour**]

- We've got to pay the salaries on Friday but the bank won't extend our overdraft. Somehow, we've got to raise the cash straight away in order to *save the situation*.

- The two executives could not agree as to who was responsible for the cash shortfall and it looked as if the police would have to be called. Luckily, the accounts section came up with an answer just in time and *the situation was saved*.
- *So, you want us to help your company out of its difficulties by lending you money, but you're not prepared to give us a stake. Putting it differently, you expect us *to save the day* for you and get nothing in return.
- **Declining product quality and poor after-sales service, have resulted in the company *losing* a good deal of *face* with its customers.

a snap (decision) a (decision) taken quickly, often in response to an urgent situation, where not enough time is given to weigh up all relevant factors and possible results

- The government's military success led to a *snap election* in hopes of an easy victory while public opinion was on their side.
- The risks involved in this project have been clear from the outset – we simply cannot make *snap decisions*, everything has to be carefully thought out.

the tip of the iceberg the small, visible, part of something much larger, the greater part of which cannot be seen [Note: often used with negative meaning]

- Once we get a foothold in our competitor's share of the market, that could be just *the tip of the iceberg*, but we have to make sure that they don't do the same to us.
- The recent financial scandal on the stock market stands to be just *the tip of the iceberg*.

without fail this is one hundred per cent sure or necessary

- A good deal of money, some SF30k in all, is missing from the company account. This is a very serious matter and we must get to the bottom of it *without fail*.
- Nine times out of ten, the managing director arrives at the office by 0800 *without fail*, so if he's late, then there must be some good reason.
- We can accept your offer, on condition that you can guarantee seven-day delivery *without fail*.

worth (doing) or **worth it** or **worthwhile** likely to pay useful dividends in return for time or effort spent

- This seems a good idea – *worth* a try, anyway.
- If something is *worth doing*, it's *worth doing* well.
- Before we go ahead with this scheme, it would be *worthwhile* having the documents checked over by the legal department.
- There are so many dead ends in this research, sometimes it seems that it just isn't *worth it*.

16 Positive Results

STUDY UNIT

to bear fruit to produce a result

- After ten years' hard work, his research finally *bore fruit*, in the shape of a revolutionary new motor.
- If discussion between the two companies *bears fruit*, as seems likely, the resulting merger will bring about far-reaching changes in the video industry.

(the) end product the final result, after completion of some process or a series of actions

- *The end product* of the negotiations was a contract between the two companies.
- Whether we buy coal from Australia or the US, either way *the end product* is the same: we're importing coal.
- Careful preparation of a presentation will lead to a more effective *end product*.

for sale on the market and available, or open, to offers to buy [Note: do not use **on sale**, which has different meanings in the US and UK]

- We're looking for new offices in the city centre. Can you look into it for us and let us know what's *for sale* or for rent at the moment.
- Thank you for your offer, but my shares in the company are not *for sale*.

in the black operating in credit, in profit, or with a (cash) surplus; with (current) assets in excess of (current) liabilities

- Shareholders will be pleased to hear that, once again, the company's year-end results show us strongly *in the black*.
- We're *in the black* on paper but not, I think, in reality – some of our assets are overvalued.

to make a profit to sell something for more than it costs to produce [Opposite in meaning to to make a loss – see Unit 17] [Note: *profit-making* can be used as an adjective*]

- The company *made an* overall *profit* on its operations last year.
- We are in business in order to *make a profit*. If we continue to employ you, we'll soon be making a loss.
- *Most of our activities are *profit-making*, although we do occasionally make a loss in some areas.
- At one time the company was highly successful but it *hasn't made a profit* for the last four years. So, what has gone wrong?

to make money to get, obtain or gain money through some activity [Note: *money-making* can also be used as an adjective as in *money-making ideas*; and as a noun as in 'This product is a good *money-maker*.'] [Opposite in meaning to to lose money, which has no noun or adjective form]

- The idea is a good one, but <u>the acid test</u> is whether it's *going to make money* <u>in practice</u>.
- <u>As yet</u>, the project *hasn't made* any *money*, but we are hoping it <u>will bear fruit</u>, <u>in the shape of</u> a reasonable profit, <u>in the</u> fairly near <u>future</u>.
- <u>The fact of the matter is that</u> the company *hasn't been making* so much *money* recently. The share price is down and we could become a target for a takeover bid.
- As you know, we *made* <u>a great deal of</u> *money* last year and, <u>according to</u> sales figures <u>so far</u>, <u>in all probability</u> we're going to <u>do the same</u> this year.

to make ... work to put and keep something in satisfactory working order or condition, to make something operative

- Although we <u>checked</u> the machine <u>over in detail</u>, we couldn't *make* it *work*. It started a few times and stopped, then finally <u>went dead</u> altogether.
- This new system is vital for the company – we have to *make* it *work*.
- These proposals can *be made to work* <u>in practice</u>, but only <u>as long as</u> we're in full agreement.

to pay dividends to produce good results

- The company's investment in staff training schemes should *pay* future *dividends* <u>in the shape of</u> more efficient, more effective personnel.
- Our research and development programme is expensive, certainly, but can be expected *to pay dividends* <u>in terms of</u> maintaining and improving our position in a competitive market.
- The chairman's recent visit to Brazil *has paid* unexpected *dividends* <u>in the shape</u> of a profitable new contract.
- A politician should be careful to make the right kind of friendships; those which are likely *to pay dividends* <u>in terms of</u> influence.

to pay (one's) way to produce enough money to cover or pay one's operating or running expenses

- The new equipment *should be paying* its *way* within a few months, <u>allowing for</u> the improved output and reduced staffing levels involved.
- Before state-owned industries can be sold to the public through privatisation, they must first be shown to be, if not actually <u>making a profit</u>, <u>at least</u> *paying* their *way*.
- Your department *is not paying* its *way*. Unless you make cuts and improve performance, you'll have to go. I'm afraid that's <u>the price you pay</u> for the privilege of being head of department.

to pull off <u>to carry out</u> successfully, using skill and/or persistence, in spite of all difficulties

- After a long battle, we *have* finally *pulled off* our takeover bid for the company.
- In the last few decades, both Germany and Japan have *pulled off* economic miracles.
- I see from the financial press that our main competitor has won a major overseas contract. I wonder how they managed to *pull it off*.

to take effect to become effective or operational in fact; to have, or show, the (intended) result of some plan or action

- Your breach of contract is so serious that it <u>rules out</u> any possibility of <u>doing</u> further <u>business with</u> you. Needless to say, the contract may be regarded as terminated, such termination *to take* immediate *effect*.
- Your promotion *will take effect* as of today, and you will, as a matter of course, be given a bigger company car <u>in lieu of</u> your present one. This is <u>in line with</u> company policy.

Evaluation and Action

STORYLINE UPDATE

As we have seen, Boldmere PLC, a company which specialises in electronic security systems, is the owner of a provisional patent on a vehicle anti-theft system called Auto Security Net (ASN), which it wishes to market. Decisions on finance and marketing taken *at the outset* can be found on page 12, along with relevant graphics. The company's proposals for finance, which were *agreed to* by its bankers, are contained in Boldmere's letter on page 29. The board, *consisting of* Jack Wagner (Chief Executive), Julia Van der Merwe (Marketing Director), Narinder Dhillon (Technical Director) and Norman Buchan (Finance Director) then *thrashed out* marketing and development strategy, which is contained *in detail* in the *game plan* on page 41.

Initial *steps have been taken with regard to* obtaining an operating licence from the Department of Trade and Industry. At the same time, Narinder Dhillon has been making a series of technical demonstrations to the police and motor insurers. It now remains to present the product to the market and *break the ice* with Saturn, the telecommunications company, to persuade them to allow Boldmere to *tie in* ASN *with* Saturn's existing network . . .

❶ WARM-UP

Do you think that Boldmere's *game plan*, and the *action taken so far*, are *on the right lines*? If not, what do you suggest?

STORYLINE

The response to the technical demonstrations was, *on the whole*, positive as you can see from the two letters received.

Metropolitan Police
Police Headquarters
59 The Lane
Beaconsfield
London N5 3FC
Phone 071 464 3333

Boldmere plc
76 Blackstock Road
Finsbury Park, London N4 6QA

3 July 19--

Dear Sirs

Re: AUTO SECURITY NET

I am directed to write on behalf of the Commissioner of Police for The Metropolis with regard to the technical demonstration of the above system which took place on 19 June.

First and foremost I have to state that it remains to be seen whether in practice the system would have any, or any significant, impact on vehicle thefts or result in higher rates of recovery of stolen vehicles. However, a first impression of the product as such is that it appears viable in principle. It is noted that further in-depth testing is to be carried out in the near future. As previously indicated, this Division is willing to assist up to a point, depending of course on availability of staff and equipment.

I should mention in passing that, in accordance with policy guidelines, it is not as a rule appropriate for any police authority publicly to endorse commercial products for whatever purpose, on the grounds that to do so would be contrary to the public interest. While such policy must hold good in this case, any legitimate means of assisting crime prevention or detection would be viewed favourably.

It is hoped that you will be able to proceed accordingly in the light of these remarks.

Yours faithfully

D. J. O'Connell

Chief Inspector D. J. O'Connell
Metropolitan Police (Traffic Division)

Lloyds-Dunbar
59–63 Pickering House
Sangford Road
London   SW5 9LE
(081) 6429851

Boldmere plc
76 Blackstock Road
London N4 6QA

26 June 19--

Dear Sirs

ASN VEHICLE ANTI-THEFT SYSTEM

We refer to the recent demonstration of this device which, on the whole, we go along with, in principle. However, we think you will agree that while the system in itself looks promising, we must surely have doubts about its effectiveness in reality on the basis of only one small-scale demonstration. That is to say, there is as yet no evidence that the system will bring about any major reduction in motor theft claims. As you will appreciate, this is the all-important factor to be taken into account by our actuaries when assessing motor premiums. In addition, as we understand it the system is to operate, at least at first, in the Greater London area only, which could give rise to further problems in calculating premiums. We do not rule out the possibility of cooperating with you but at the moment we feel on balance that we cannot run unnecessary risks on behalf of our members, whose interests must take first place.

In essence we are prepared to look further into the matter but we have to make sure that there is a realistic prospect that the system will bear fruit in the shape of fewer claims on this company. For this reason we have to reserve final judgement for the time being. If, however, you are able to take your recent demonstration one step further by setting up a larger-scale dummy run, this could put us more in the picture as to how our members and policyholders might benefit from the end product.
   We look forward to hearing from you.

Yours faithfully

F. D. Tootle

For and on behalf of CYGNET MOTOR POLICIES AT LLOYDS-DUNBAR

❷ WORD STUDY

What is the meaning of the words/expressions listed below, which you will find in the two letters? Show that you know the meaning of the words by using them in short sentences.

a. viable
b. indicated
c. willing
d. assist
e. staff
f. appropriate
g. endorse
h. contrary to the public interest
i. legitimate
j. means
k. detection
l. viewed favourably
m. proceed

n. device
o. promising
p. effectiveness
q. evidence
r. theft
s. claim
t. appreciate
u. actuary
v. assessing
w. premium
x. reserve final judgement
y. members
z. policyholders

❸ WORD STUDY

Rewrite the following sentences, replacing the words in brackets with words from the box below. Put the words into their correct form where necessary.

to handle	tough	to think up	site-sharing	accessory	market
projection	provisional	to be caught up	package	scheme	
concrete	to promote	target	outcome		

a. The company has made a profits (prediction based on available information) but the (result) will not be known until the year-end balance sheet is prepared.

b. We obtained (temporary or conditional) agreement for (joint use of a piece of land) with the TV company.

c. It is a (very difficult) job, but we can (deal with) it.

d. They are (trapped) in a loveless marriage.

e. They (*came up with*) a (definite) (plan) to (encourage the sale of) the product to the (intended) (group of potential customers).

f. In an effort to boost sales, motor manufacturers are to offer customers a (a set of items to be offered *for sale* together as a single unit), including discounts of up to thirty per cent on (extra or accompanying items to be used with a main item to improve usefulness or appearance).

> ## STORYLINE
>
> Boldmere have now been *in touch with* the telecom company and with the government department concerned with issuing the necessary licence to operate the scheme. The Boldmere team are to meet to discuss the present position and *to think over the next step.*

❹ TRANSFER

Imagine you are to attend Boldmere's next meeting. Prepare a brief written report of results achieved *so far*, refer to the *game plan*, identify and summarise any problems and make recommendations for *action to be taken*.

❺ WORD STUDY

Match the half sentences in the left-hand column with the correct half on the right in order to make a full sentence. The first one is done for you.

a. I'm afraid I don't agree	**1.** *in lieu*?
b. The bank refuses to accept instalments, they want payment	**2.** it's *a safe bet* he'll be dead within a year.
c. We can't give you $US for your yen, will you accept Swiss Francs	**3.** we *stand to make a large profit*.
d. If he carries on drinking a bottle of whisky a day,	**4.** *at all*.
e. If share prices continue rising,	**5.** *in full, at once*.

❻ LISTENING · NOTE-TAKING

 Now listen to the meeting and make notes about what has been done *so far* and what is proposed for the future. Compare these notes with your own report which you wrote in Question 4. (Note: the speakers will use the words from the box in Question 3.)

❼ COMPREHENSION

a. What did Evelyn George do that helped Narinder Dhillon *make his point* during the technical demonstration?

b. What does Jack Wagner say should be done *in the short term*?

c. What problems or dangers does Norman Buchan foresee?

d. What does he suggest needs to be done?

e. What does Julia Van der Merwe say needs to be done?

f. What specific action does she propose?

g. What kind of information do you think Julia Van der Merwe should produce in response to Jack Wagner's final question?

After the meeting, Norman Buchan produced the following memorandum.

Boldmere plc

From: Norman Buchan

To: Jack Wagner/Julia Van der Merwe

Re: Tuesday's meeting – ASN

I have two suggestions to make from my standpoint as Finance Director. I hope these will be useful.

1. Saturn: As yet we cannot justify the expense of a full site sharing agreement. On the other hand we need the use of some at least of Saturn's facilities in order to set up a dry run of ASN for the police, insurers, motor manufacturers and so on. I therefore recommend that we aim at negotiating an option for a full site sharing agreement. This would involve:

- a right to instal equipment and use Saturn facilities for the purpose of carrying out testing
- a period long enough for us to put the system to the acid test
- a fixed fee, to be offset against the full agreement fee if we go ahead with full site sharing
- terms of site-sharing being agreed in full, but so that the agreement need not take effect unless and until the system can be made to work to everyone's satisfaction and so that we can go ahead or not at will.

If we are able to make a deal on this basis then we cut our losses in case things go wrong and we are not running unnecessary risks with shareholders' money – at most we stand to lose the option fee.

2. Costing: Earlier projections allow for installation costs but do not take into account any premium reductions – as a sweetener to the market – which in any case are a means to an end, although by the same token they could help buoy up the price. In the light of the fact that ASN is still at the testing stage, we can only quote rough price guidelines based on current projections – anything else could only be on a hit and miss basis, it's as simple as that, I'm afraid. I suggest that we avoid talking about price but that in the last resort, if our back is against the wall, we have no choice but to quote on current projections but must make it clear that these may be subject to change.

n

❽ WORD STUDY

In the left-hand column, below, are some words/expressions from Buchan's memorandum. From the list on the right, find the word or expression closest in meaning.

a. standpoint	**1.** investors in a company
b. facilities	**2.** to raise or support
c. option	**3.** incentive or persuasion
d. offset	**4.** means or equipment to help the progress of some action
e. fee	**5.** step or period of development
f. shareholders	**6.** physical or mental position from which things are seen
g. sweetener	**7.** to state a price
h. buoy up	**8.** approximate
i. stage	**9.** payment for services
j. quote	**10.** a right obtained and paid for to do something in the future
k. rough	**11.** general idea or principle to lead or control actions
l. guidelines	**12.** on condition that
m. subject to	**13.** to counterbalance or compensate

STORYLINE

Norman Buchan's memorandum was discussed at a further meeting. The following memorandum from Jack Wagner summarises the position after the second meeting.

Boldmere plc

From: JW

To: JM/NB

Re: ASN

To summarise the present position after our meetings on Tuesday and Friday:
1. In the light of the response to technical demonstrations, we stand a reasonable chance of getting a provisional licence from the DTI.
2. But, by the same token, it is clear that we will have to arrange for a medium to large scale dry run of the system for both the police, insurers and the target market, that is, motor manufacturers and accessory dealers.
3. In turn, this cannot be set up except in conjunction with Saturn.

4. On the other hand, we have to keep an eye on costs: as yet, a full site-sharing agreement with Saturn would be taking too much of a chance.

5. However, we are running behind schedule and in any case we need to get in touch with the market to test the reaction to ASN before making a site-sharing deal with Saturn.

6. On that basis, the following action to be taken:
   - JW to deal with licence application to DTI
   - JW to approach Saturn and set up a meeting (also with NB) to negotiate an option on the lines set out in NB's memo
   - JM (with ND) to arrange for presentation/technical demos to the market.

Each of these steps depends on the others – any dead ends could result in reaching a stalemate or, as has been mentioned, being caught up in a vicious circle. So it goes without saying that we must take care to work closely hand in hand with each other – this is a matter of make or break.

J

❾ WORD STUDY

In the following text, replace the expressions in brackets with one of the expressions from the box below.

in the light of	by the same token	on that basis	set out
depends on	it goes without saying	on the lines	

TO ALL STAFF – DAMAGE TO EQUIPMENT

((a) The fact is so obvious and it is not really necessary to mention) that the efficiency of this company ((b) is very uncertain without) all staff cooperating ((c) according to the procedures) ((d) explained in detail) in the 'Company Guidelines' booklet. ((e) Because of what is now clear from) recent events all staff are reminded to take care when using equipment so that it does not *go out of action in the first place*, and *in particular* to make sure that any problems or *breakdowns* are reported *at once*. ((f) In accordance with this standard) equipment can be kept in good working order and ((g) for the same reason) general efficiency in the company can be maintained.

🔟 LISTENING

Listen to the following telephone conversation between Jack Wagner and Cynthia King of Saturn.

⑪ ORAL TRANSFER

Imagine that you are Cynthia King and make an oral summary of the conversation to your secretary for noting on file.

⑫ WRITTEN TRANSFER

Now imagine you are Jack Wagner and write a short memorandum for Norman Buchan and Julia Van der Merwe, telling them what you proposed, how Cynthia King reacted and what the outcome of the conversation was.

⑬ READING

The following text is part of a lecture on company finance (the next part is in Practice Section E). What is the meaning of the underlined words and expressions? Show that you know the meaning by using them in short sentences.

Financial problems can come up for a variety of reasons, for example: rising overheads, failure to meet budgets, or due to bad debts which have to be written off. A company may also find itself in difficulty through diversification – that is to say, branching out into new areas of business, which can result in overspending and underfunding if not properly controlled. These problems can have far-reaching consequences ... .

Negative Results

STUDY UNIT 17

to be (or **go**) **out of action** to not work or operate; to fail to function or to stop working / operating / functioning

- The computer's *out of action* at the moment, due to an electrical fault.
- What! The *photocopier's gone out of action* again? What's the problem this time?
- The meeting has to be cancelled, as the chairman's *out of action* – too much champagne last night!

to break down to fail; to collapse; to stop [Also means to destroy or overcome** and to present in detail***] [Note: *breakdown* can be used as a noun* and as an adjective as in a *breakdown* truck]

- The first two negotiations were unsuccessful and the third *broke down* after only a few hours.
- The photocopier *has broken down* again. It may be due to overheating, or it could be mechanical failure.
- *The sales manager's problems at work stem from, or were maybe brought about by, *the breakdown* of his marriage.
- **In spite of careful promotion, the new product came up against strong market resistance, which we were unable to *break down*.
- ***This balance sheet does not give enough information. We need a complete *breakdown* of the figures.

(a) dead end a path going nowhere; a direction or course from which there is no exit or which results in no progress [Note: *dead-end* can be used as a noun or an adjective*]

- The research programme had looked promising, but all the tests led to *dead ends*.
- *After five years without promotion, she felt she was in *a dead-end* job.
- *He had not produced any artwork for some years and felt that he had come to *a creative *dead end*.

dud not performing the required or expected function; ineffective in result or effect [Note: *dud* can be used as a noun or an adjective] [informal]

- We had high expectations of your assistant, but it seems he's turned out to be *a dud* on the job, in spite of all his qualifications.
- How can we be expected to carry out our jobs with the *dud* equipment you gave us?
- The meeting was *a* complete *dud* – only three people turned up.

to go dead (on) to stop working, responding or developing

- The fax machine's broken down. I don't know what went wrong; one moment it was working and, the next, it just *went dead*.
- We negotiated with them for months. They seemed interested at first and then they *went dead on* us – no replies to phone calls and faxes, no letters, nothing.
- A presenter's nightmare is when your audience *goes dead on* you.

to go wrong to make a mistake; to miscalculate or misjudge; to develop negative characteristics.

- When carrying out this experiment, it is important to remember above all to be

67

exact and go step by step and not cut corners. If you *go wrong*, the results can be expensive, and dangerous. So, better safe than sorry.

- Ah, yes, I can see at a glance where you *went wrong* in your calculations. You've added an extra zero, making 100 into 1,000.

in the red operating in debit, at a loss, or with a (cash) deficit; with (current) liabilities in excess of (current) assets

- 'The bank manager's on the phone. He says it's about our overdraft.'
  'Oh, really? He should be used to us being *in the red* by now so what's he getting so excited about, I wonder?'
- The company's final results put it seriously *in the red* and a sharp fall in its share price has taken place.

in vain unsuccessfully; without reaching one's objective; with no result

- The managers tried to save the company, but *in vain*. Within six months it went out of business.
- For months we've been trying *in vain* to persuade them to agree to our proposals and now, suddenly, they've agreed to everything.
- OK, so the project wasn't a success, but all our efforts haven't been entirely *in vain*. We've collected a lot of useful data and, what's more, we can learn from our mistakes.
- HAVE TRIED CONTACTING YOU BY PHONE **IN VAIN** – PLS REPLY THIS TLX ASAP TO CONFIRM FLIGHT NUMBER AND ETA BOMBAY

to make a loss to sell something for less than its production cost [Opposite in meaning to to make a profit] [Note: *loss-making* can be used as an adjective*, and is also used as a noun as in 'This product is a *lossmaker*.']

- Expenditure last year was $HK8m and income $HK7.3m, so the company *made a loss* of $HK0.7m.
- Forecasts show that we stand to *make a loss* on our US business during the company's current financial year.

- *The company would be a more attractive investment without its *loss-making* overseas activities.

to pay the penalty (or **price**) **for** to suffer the negative result of one's actions

- If we don't invest in new equipment, we*'ll pay the penalty for* it later in terms of loss of production.
- The young executive *paid the penalty for* spending too much time on business; his wife left him for another man.
- He invested funds with an unknown investment company which promised high returns on unlisted securities. Not surprisingly, he *paid a* heavy *price for* doing so. When the company went bankrupt, he lost everything.
- Time and money spent on training is *a small price to pay for* the dividends it would pay the company in terms of increasing staff effectiveness.
- In this company, staff have to work long hours, but *that's the price you pay for* the high salary and benefits.
- European political union would have many advantages, but there is a strong argument that the resulting loss of autonomy of member states would be *too high a price to pay*.

to reach a stalemate (in negotiations, etc) to arrive at a position where no progress can be made, where neither side can win or lose [Also **to reach a deadlock***]

- Talks between the two governments were broken off when *a stalemate was reached*.

- Negotiations for the merger of the two companies were called off after accountants *reached a stalemate* over valuation of assets.
- *Discussions are now being held with a view to breaking through *the deadlock reached* at last week's meeting.

to be (or **to fall**) **short of** to be less than needed, wanted or expected; to lack something; to not be enough [Note: *shortfall* can be used as a noun*]

- The test results are interesting as far as they go, but they *fall* far *short of* proving the safety of this product.
- *Although gross profit, as such, is higher than forecast, net profit figures show *a shortfall* on projections – SF8m, to be exact.
- At first sight, the new manager seemed able to cope with his responsibilities. Under the acid test of stress, however, his performance *fell* seriously *short*.
- Evidence from the public enquiry arising from last year's riots has produced a number of hard facts. First and foremost, it is now crystal clear that government statements at the time *fell* considerably *short of* the truth. This credibility gap is likely to prove a drawback to the government at the next election.

to take the consequences to accept the (negative) results of some (risky or foolish) action

- Taking risks also involves *taking the consequences* if things go wrong.
- Management made a series of errors and must now *take the consequences* of those errors in the shape of reduced benefits.

(a) vicious circle a negative situation in which any action leads only to further negative results

- Diversification by a company, in terms of its marketing aims, must be carefully thought out as branching out can produce a *vicious circle* of overspending, underfunding, failure to meet objectives, falling standards and declining custom, all leading at the end of the day to bankruptcy.
- Companies continuing to produce goods in a dying market are creating a *vicious circle*.

STUDY UNIT

Tactics

to back down to show a marked change of attitude or position, from being in confrontation to being passive, neutral or accepting; to withdraw

- After days of hard negotiating, both sides *backed down* sufficiently in their demands to make agreement possible.
- Critics of the new process *backed down* completely after tests showed that it was not dangerous, as they had previously believed.

to back out (of) to fail to carry out (or to withdraw from) some promise, arrangement, agreement or obligation [Also means to reverse a motor vehicle from a garage or driveway]

- The agreement had been drawn up and we were about to sign when we heard that the other party had *backed out* at the last moment.
- You can rely on her for sure. Once she agrees to do something, she never *backs out of it.*

to break off to end suddenly [Also means to pause in speaking or working] [Note: also noun form *breaking off**]

- *The *breaking off* of diplomatic relations between two countries may signal the start of warfare.
- Negotiations between the two companies, which had already begun to break down over disagreement about product quality, *were* finally *broken off* when prices could not be agreed.

to keep (one's) options open to decide against taking any firm decision now, in favour of keeping a free choice for later

- We've not yet decided where to relocate our factories. A number of possibilities are being investigated and we're *keeping our options open* for the time being.
- In deciding neither for nor against selling off state-controlled companies, the government is clearly *keeping its options open.*

to lay (it) on the line to speak clearly and frankly; to make one's position obvious [Also **to spell (it) out***]

- I'm *laying it on the line* to you – either you improve your performance or you'll get no annual bonus; it's as simple as that.
- We've got to *lay our position clearly on the line* at the meeting. There must be no misunderstanding.
- *You clearly haven't understood what I've been saying. Let me *spell it out* for you: either you deliver the goods by tomorrow or you can treat our contract as at an end.

to mean business to be serious or determined in executing some intention; to be purposeful

- Right from the start of this negotiation, we have to let the other side know that we really *mean business.*
- Recent discussions broke the ice with this potential customer. What's more, after our recent sales presentation, they're showing real interest in our products. It's beginning to look as if they *mean business.*
- The new company logo is designed on purpose to show that we *mean business.*

to play ball (with) to cooperate or negotiate with a view to doing business or reaching some agreement [informal]

- After months of refusing to back down from their original demands, the two governments have at last agreed to *play ball*.
- Our marketing game plan looks as if it's going to pay dividends. We've had a strong response from companies wanting to *play ball with* us.
- If you're prepared *to play ball* as to price, then we can *play ball* as to the size of orders.

to put (the) pressure on to try to improve one's position by use of persistence, forcefulness or threats

- In business, as in sport or war, when you can see that your opponent is tired, that's the time to *put the pressure on*.
- Our department *has been putting pressure on* the company for months for further headcount, but so far in vain.
- They are not prepared to see reason, so we'll have to *put pressure on* them if we want to succeed.

to rely on to depend on; to trust

- You can *rely on* us to deliver on time.
- These customers just can't *be relied on* at all these days; their invoice payments are getting later and later.

- Our reputation rests on the fact that customers know they can *rely on* our products.

to soften up to reduce resistance or to weaken opposition or hostility in order to achieve an objective more easily [Note: the noun form, *softening up**, can also be used adjectivally, as in a *softening-up* process]

- The speaker could sense the audience's hostility, so he tried *softening* them *up* with a few jokes before starting on his main theme.
- Before a new product is launched on the market, potential buyers may need to *be softened up* by use of marketing techniques to make the product seem attractive.
- *You can expect a very tough attitude from the trade union representative. He'll need some *softening up* if there's to be any chance at all of your proposal being accepted.

to stand (or stick) out for to be firmly decided not to accept less than one wants, even if it means waiting for it [Also **to hold out for***]

- We've decided not to accept the offer of SF50k. *We're standing out for* the original SF58k asking price.
- *Having stuck out for* their demands for so long, the unions are expected to reject management's latest offer.
- *The house has been for sale for over a year without a buyer. We can't continue *holding out* for the asking price.

to take a (firm) line (or stand) on/over to show a (determined) intention, attitude or approach

- These customers are once again behind schedule with their loan repayments. We'll have to *take a firm line* with them.
- We have to try to talk the sales director out of resigning; but what is *the best line to take*?
- Staff are spending too much time going back and forth to the canteen. It's got to be ruled out, I'm afraid. We'll have to *take a firm line* and make it crystal clear that anyone found wasting time will have his or her pay docked.

to talk (someone) out of to use argument or discussion to persuade someone not to do something

- The customer insisted on driving us to the airport but of course he wasn't fit to drive as he had been drinking. So we had to *talk* him *out of* it by telling him that a taxi had already been ordered.
- We had intended selling some company land in order to raise extra money, but our financial adviser *talked* us *out of* it.

to talk (someone) round to persuade someone to change an attitude, intention or decision [Also means to avoid speaking directly about something*]

- He's a difficult man to deal with. Once he's made his mind up *there's no talking him round*, and no amount of softening up will enable you to talk him out of doing what he wants.

- The unions are threatening a strike. We'll have to *talk* them *round* fast, otherwise we'll never finish production on that large order in time.
- *Can we stop *talking round* the problem and come to the point?

to withdraw (from) to leave or move away from an unsatisfactory or dangerous situation [Note: the noun form is *withdrawal**]

- Unless agreement can be reached today, we *will withdraw from* the negotiations.
- If the bank *withdrew* our financial backing, we would have to find other means of financing our operations.
- Two of our overseas representatives *will* have to *be withdrawn* in order to cut costs.
- *Heavy losses led to the *withdrawal of* British banks and insurance companies from the US market.

19 Attitudes Opinions and Discussion

to argue against to oppose with logic [Note: opposite in meaning to **to argue in favour of**]

- The Research and Development Manager *argued* strongly *against* reducing his department's annual budget.
- The trade union representatives *argued against* company proposals to replace sixty per cent of the workforce with machinery.

to be against to oppose; to be opposed or contrary to [Note: opposite in meaning to to be for or to be in favour of]

- This company *is against* joint venture schemes because experience shows that these so often go wrong.
- *We're not against* your proposals as such, on the contrary we think they look very interesting on paper, but we think they need to be carefully looked into before we decide if we can play ball with you.
- On checking over the scheme in detail, we take the view that it *would be against* our interests to go ahead. We should back out now.

the ball is in (your) court it's up to (you) to take action; the next step is for (you) to take; (we) await your next move

- We've made them a good offer – now *the ball's in their court.*
- *The Committee of Enquiry made its recommendations clear to the government – now the ball is firmly in the government's court.*

to change (one's) mind to change a decision or opinion

- 'I'm afraid we're not now able to go ahead with our arrangement to do business with your company. For reasons of policy, which I can't explain, *we've changed our mind.*'
  'You mean, someone has made you a better offer so you've decided to back out of our contract.'
- At first, she didn't like her new colleague at all, but after a while she *changed her mind.*

the facts speak for themselves the known facts of a situation clearly show the answers to any questions about them

- The company's financial records told the whole story. We could see at a glance that large sums were not accounted for. *The facts spoke for themselves* – this was a case of fraud.
- Anyone who doubts the quality of our products is invited to test them and let *the facts speak for themselves.*
- 'Why do you think the company is in trouble?'
  'Because, according to the latest accounts, profits are falling, the share price is down and borrowings are too high as well. *The facts speak for themselves.*'

to get across (to) to communicate; to make clear; to reach

- I'm trying *to get across to* you that I'm very worried about our financial position but you're just not taking the point.
- When making a presentation, it is necessary to decide what ideas or information one wants to *get across*.
- *We're not getting across to* each other at all, in fact, we're talking at cross purposes.
- Her open, friendly manner and professional approach enable her to *get herself across* effectively *to* our clients.

to get (one's) priorities (right) to choose the (correct) order of priorities, values, actions according to circumstances

- Time management is largely a matter of *getting one's priorities right*, that is to say deciding what must be done, what should be done and what one would like to do.
- Look, we seem to be talking at cross purposes. I think we should *get our priorities straight* before we continue.
- No, no, you're concentrating on the last stage of the process, when you should be thinking about the first step. *You've got your priorities all wrong*.

to (have) an open mind to be mentally flexible, to be ready and able to receive, process and (if necessary) adapt to new or opposing ideas or views. [Note: The adjective form is *open-minded**]

- It is all-important in the business world to approach sensible propositions *with an open mind*.
- Please don't be afraid to speak freely. In this company we *keep an open mind* on new ideas – as long as they agree with our own, of course!
- *The foreign government's representative *was* surprisingly *open-minded* about our proposals. We had expected an unfriendly response.

in (my) opinion (I) take the view that; my skill or experience leads me to believe that [Also **in my view***]

- The lawyer, after considering all the facts, said that *in her opinion*, her client

company stood a reasonable chance of success in the lawsuit.

- *In the opinion of* some financial journalists, the company could be a target for a takeover bid.
- *Although some of you may disagree, *in my own view* we should delay our decision until the end of the week.

to insist on to press or impose one's actions, wishes or views on others [Note: also noun form *insistence on**]

- We must *insist on* immediate payment of our invoice, before despatch of the next consignment under the contract.
- *Your boss's *insistence on* getting drunk at the reception caused the company considerable embarrassment.

to make (one's) point to succeed in making understood the logic or sense of an argument or opinion

- The aim of a presentation is *to make one's point* efficiently and effectively.
- 'Your performance so far is not quite in line with what we expect from our executives – I hope I*'ve made my point*?' 'Yes! In a word you want to see some improvements, and, if not . . .'. 'Exactly. . .'.
- Well done! You *made your point* very well at the meeting and I'm sure many of us agreed with you.
- During the discussion, the finance director *made the point* that shareholders' expectation of dividends had to be taken into account.
- If I can just interrupt for a moment, I'd like to *make the point* that as a rule we don't lend sums in excess of DM3m, although that, in itself, does not mean we can't do business with you.

to make clear to explain so that there can be no possibility of misunderstanding

- The company's attitude towards its shareholders *was made clear* in the chairman's annual report today.
- Our position *was made* perfectly *clear* to you at the start of these negotiations, so you cannot now say you misunderstood.
- We *have made* our offer in absolutely

clear terms, so the ball is now very much in your court.

a matter of fact something known or proved, or believed by the speaker, to be true or correct [Note: the adjectival form is *matter-of-fact**]

- It's *a matter of* commercial *fact* that every product has a limited lifespan.
- 'Do you have the sales figures?' 'As *a matter of fact*, I don't. I gave them to the boss.'
- *He was a clever persuader, telling lies in such a *matter-of-fact* way that many people believed him and invested their money in his company.

to point out to show or indicate; to make clear; to emphasise

- The presenter *pointed out* to the audience the important features of the new product.
- If I can interrupt for a moment, may I just *point out* that the sales figures we've just seen do not take into account the large order received at the end of the month.
- We made our offer three weeks ago and they haven't replied. I think we have to *point out* to them that if they want to play ball, they need to let us know more or less at once

to put the record straight to put right any misunderstandings; to correct any false ideas by giving the true facts

- First of all, let me *put the record straight*; whatever rumours you may have heard, it is not my government's intention to raise import duties on foreign goods.
- I think we have to *put the record straight*; your company and mine have been dissatisfied with one another for some time, although nothing has been said openly, and it's time things were thrashed out.

to (be) take(n) aback to (be) cause(d) a feeling of surprise or astonishment, often also with disappointment or dismay

- We had fully expected a positive response from them so we *were* considerably *taken aback* by their rejection of our terms.

- I had not expected his plan to succeed, so I *was not* at all *taken aback* to learn of the disappointing results.
- News of the police investigation into company affairs *took* everyone *aback*.

to take the long view to form a decision or opinion based not only on the present position but also taking into account long-term developments

- In the main, good quality products last much longer, but are more expensive than those of poor quality. So, *taking the long view*, it's worthwhile buying them, although you need enough money in the first place.
- I know some of you think this proposal doesn't make sense. From a short-term view, I take your point. However, *I'm taking the long view* that taking this step will prove most beneficial in the long term.

to take the view (that) to have or be of the opinion (that)

- I *take the view that* we have reached a stalemate and should withdraw from the negotiations.
- As your lawyer, I *take the view*, without prejudice to your legal rights, *that* on balance you ought to compromise with the insurance company over your claim and make do with their offer of eighty per cent of your actual loss, plus legal expenses.
- At yesterday's union meeting, *the* general *view was taken* that the company's offer with regard to redundancy pay fell short of legal requirements and that pressure should be put on the company to face up to its legal responsibilities.

to talk over (with) to discuss or consider fully, in all its aspects

- Your idea seems interesting – let's *talk* it *over*.
- We can't give a 'yes' or 'no' answer to these proposals until we've *talked them over with* our clients.
- There are a few matters I'd like to *talk over with* you. Let's go to my office, shall we?

Developing Ideas and Arguments

as we have seen as has already been shown, proved or demonstrated

- *As we have seen* from the trading figures, sales in all sectors are up, although profits remain marginal.
- Our competitors have, *as we have seen* from past experience, always been ready to cut prices in order to win a larger market share.
- The production manager cannot be relied on any longer. *As we have seen*, every order is behind schedule.

as well (as) too; also; in addition (to)

- Not only are our products the best on the market, they're reasonably priced *as well*.
- *As well as* being the best on the market, our products are also reasonably priced.

to begin (or **start**) **with** at first; first of all; at the beginning

- *To begin with*, the business grew slowly but after several years it expanded rapidly.
- *To begin with*, I'm going to tell you about sales over the past year. I'll then go on to deal with projections for the coming year.
- There are two good reasons why we have to reprimand the production manager. *To start with*, he's inefficient and, besides, he has a habit of being rude to staff.

by the same token for the same reason; as a logical extension of the same argument

- Because of falling profits, research and development costs must be drastically reduced. *By the same token*, there are to be no salary increases.
- Workers have the right to strike in support of a dispute; *by the same token*, employers have the right to dismiss them for breach of contract.
- He is a tough professional negotiator who usually gets what he wants, but *by the same token* he is not a popular man.

by the way changing the subject, incidentally, in passing

- Really? That's interesting. *By the way*, did you hear the latest news about our competitors?
- . . . about production figures. I think I should mention, *by the way*, that we have now found a replacement for the production manager. Now, to get back to what I was saying, production figures. . .

in addition (to) also; besides; over and above; too [Same as as well (as)]

- You have seen the agenda for today's meeting. *In addition*, there are some other matters which I wish to discuss.
- This machine employs the latest technology; *in addition*, it's inexpensive.

in other words saying the same thing in a different way; to summarise [Also that is to say]

- The basic function of financial institutions is to advance credit facilities; *in other words*, banks do business by lending money.
- We have doubts about the feasibility of this project; *in other words*, we don't think it's a good idea.

- Increasing interest rates has an impact on the economy; *in other words*, it brings about an increase in foreign investment while at the same time results in financial problems amongst domestic borrowers.

in passing incidentally; by the way; another important matter (not directly connected with what I am saying) is

- While we're talking about our research and development budget, I'd like to mention, *in passing*, that our competitors have increased theirs by up to thirty per cent.
- Before we discuss an extension of the contract, I would say, *in passing*, that we have had some complaints from customers who have bought your product, about quality not matching price.

in the first place first of all; for a start; as a first step; before anything else is said or done; in the first instance; to start with; to begin with; first and foremost [Note: **in the second** etc **place** is a useful variation to introduce other items in a list*]

- You now say you can't deliver on time, but you must have known this when we placed the order with you. So why didn't you tell us *in the first place*?
- If you had been more careful *in the first place*, you wouldn't have come up against these problems.
- The man was injured on the construction site but he was a visitor, not a workman, so he shouldn't have been there *in the first place*.
- *The management consultants recommended, *in the first place*, a reduction in overheads; *in the second place*, a review of the product range; and, *in the third place*, a fresh share issue.

in the same way similarly; likewise; by the same token

- For this reason, we do not agree with your first suggestion. *In the same way*, your second suggestion is also unacceptable.
- This process can be used to produce sulphuric acid. *In the same way*, it can be used to produce building plaster.

to put it (differently) to say or explain something (in a different way)

- 'You should cut spending,' advised the accountant, 'or, *to put it differently*, if you don't cut spending, you'll be in difficulties in two years' time.'
- 'Sales are not doing well at the moment?' 'That's *putting it* mildly, they're down thirty per cent.'
- 'We need complete reorganisation of our human resources.' 'I agree with you up to a point, but I think total reorganisation *is putting it* rather too *strongly*.'
- 'Do you agree with our proposals?' 'Well, let me *put it* like this – we don't entirely agree but we don't entirely disagree.'
- I don't think we should tell the sales manager to cut his entertainment budget due to falling net profits – I'm sure we can *put it another way*.
- If your job performance doesn't improve, then the company may not renew your contract. I can't *put it* more clearly than that.

what is more in addition especially; this is (even more) important

- Your employment with this company is terminated. *What's more*, I suggest you leave at once because if not, I'll call the police.
- As you can see, these figures show a rise in value of our investments. *What's more*, there is a marked increase in return on most of these investments.
- You need to improve your performance. *What's more*, we'll be keeping an eye on you to make sure you do.

A Presentation

STORYLINE UPDATE

Boldmere PLC, a company specialising in the field of electronic security systems, wishes to market Auto Security Net (ASN), a vehicle anti-theft system on which it holds a provisional patent. Finance and marketing decisions (see memo and relevant graphics on page 12) led to Boldmere's proposals for finance to its bankers (see memo on page 29) and these were agreed. The board of directors, *consisting of* Jack Wagner (Chief Executive), Julia Van der Merwe (Marketing Director), Norman Buchan (Finance Director) and Narinder Dhillon (Technical Director) then agreed their marketing and development strategy (see *game plan* on page 41).

An approach has been made to the Department of Trade and Industry (DTI) for a code operator's licence, which ASN will require. Meanwhile, Narinder Dhillon has made a series of technical demonstrations to police and motor insurers, whose cooperation is required *in order to* obtain the licence and to help market the product. However, the response received has *made it clear* that a *full-scale dry run* of the system will be required before such cooperation can be given. The Boldmere board met to discuss the situation and this led to a tactical suggestion from Norman Buchan (see memo on page 63) which was adopted as part of the overall plan (see memo on page 64).

It still remains to present the product to the market and, *above all*, to obtain the vital cooperation of Saturn, the telecommunications company, so that Boldmere can *tie* ASN *in with* Saturn's existing Greater London network.

❶ WARM-UP

What factors need *to be taken into account in connection with* making a marketing presentation?

STORYLINE

In accordance with Boldmere's marketing strategy, Julia Van der Merwe and Narinder Dhillon now begin a series of presentations to motor manufacturers and accessory dealers, followed up by technical demonstrations *on the same lines* as before. We are about to meet them at the offices of the British subsidiary of a French motor manufacturer, where Julia is to present ASN *in general terms* to Victor Decard, UK Procurements Manager, and Robert Kerner, UK Chief Engineer. First look at Diagrams A to F used in the presentation.

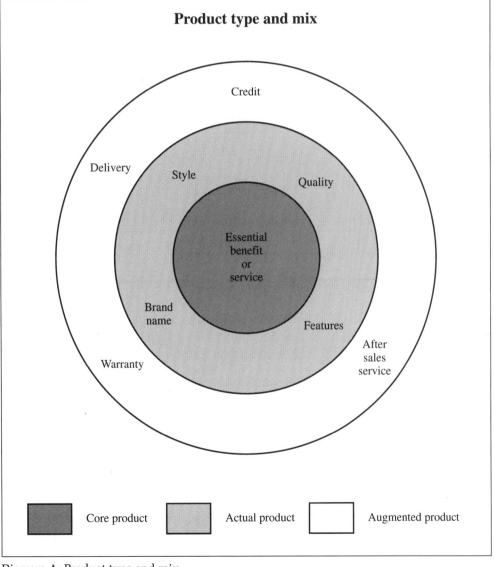

Diagram A: Product type and mix

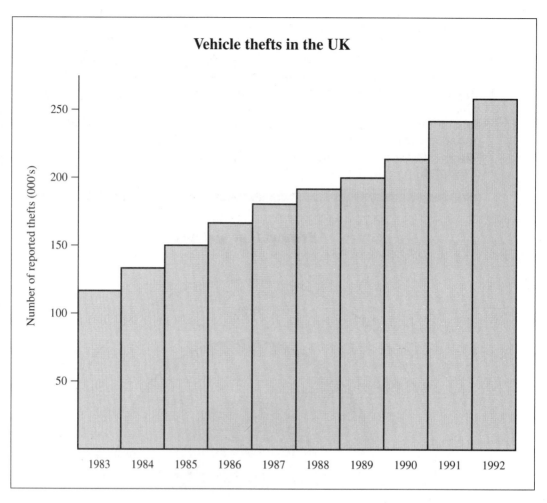

Diagram B: Vehicle thefts in the UK

Consumer attitudes: Greater London
Random sampling of 1630 adults.

- Do you own or run a vehicle?

| YES 86% | NO 14% |

- Is it fitted with an anti-theft device?

| YES 34% | NO 66% |

- If so, what kind?

Steering lock	Car alarm	Other	None
15%	29%	0%	56%

- How many people do you know who have been affected by vehicle crime in the last 10 years?

0	1	2	4	5	5+
0%	18%	23%	44%	12%	3%

- Have you had a vehicle stolen in the last ten years?

| YES 23% | NO 77% |

- If yes, was the vehicle fitted with an anti-theft device?

| YES 68% | NO 22% |

- Was the vehicle insured?

| YES 93% | NO 7% |

- Was the vehicle recovered?

| YES 22% | NO 78% |

- If not, did your insurance company pay compensation?

| YES 73% | NO 27% |

- If yes, were you satisfied with the compensation?

| YES 26% | NO 74% |

- If compensation was not paid, what reasons were given?

Lack of anti-theft precautions	Other
79%	21%

- How much has your motor insurance premium increased in the last 10 years?

Nil	0–20%	20–30%	30–50%	Over 50%
0%	0%	0%	0%	100%

- Do you know of any product on the market which would give your vehicle protection against theft, or enure its recovery if stolen?

| YES 0% | NO 100% |

- Would you be interested in such a product either as standard equipment or as an accessory?

| YES 100% | NO 0% |

Diagram C: Consumer attitudes

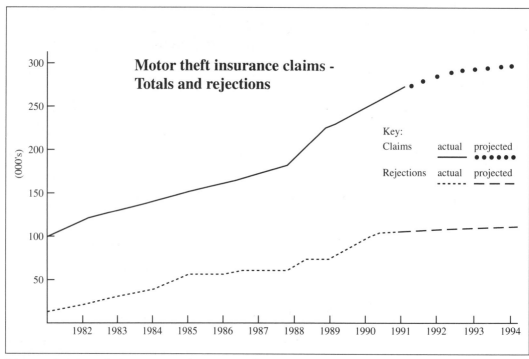

Diagram D: Motor theft insurance claims – Totals + rejections

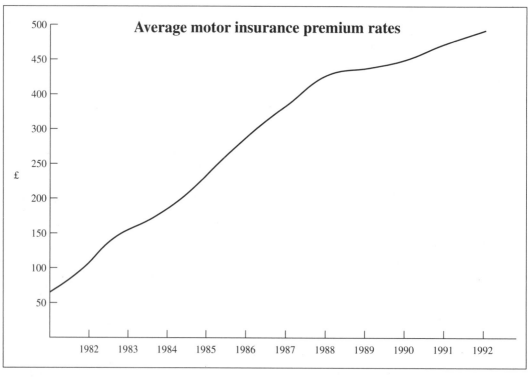

Diagram E: Average motor insurance premium rates

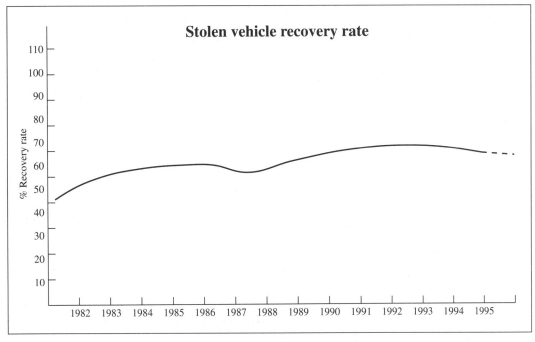

Diagram F: Stolen vehicle recovery rates

❷ LISTENING·COMPREHENSION

 Listen to Part 1 of Julia's presentation to the French motor manufacturer, and then answer the following questions.

   a. In her introduction, Julia Van der Merwe says she is going to divide her presentation into sections. What are the main areas she is going to concentrate on?

   b. In this first part of the presentation, what do you think is the most important point she is trying *to get across*?

   c. How do you think she will build on this later?

❸ TRANSFER

   a. How do you think she will develop her theme later in the presentation?

   b. Practise presenting Diagram A.

❹ WORD STUDY

What is the meaning of the following words/expressions which were used in the first part of the presentation? Show that you understand the meaning by using these words in short sentences.

   a. to hand over

   b. concepts

   c. luxury features

   d. benefits

   e. flip chart

   f. core product

   g. standard

   h. optional extras

   i. dealers

❺ LISTENING • COMPREHENSION

 Listen to an extract from Part 2 of the presentation and make notes to help you answer the following question. What arguments or tactics does Julia Van der Merwe use to persuade her audience that a recession can be the right time to market a new product?

❻ TRANSFER

Practise presenting Diagrams B, C, D and E.

❼ WORD STUDY

In the left-hand column below are some words and expressions from Part 2 of Julia Van der Merwe's presentation. From the list on the right, find the word or expression closest in meaning.

a. lazy lock	**1.** disbelieving
b. soaring	**2.** unsystematic method of testing or researching
c. stockpiles	**3.** steeply and suddenly
d. overstate the case	**4.** rapidly rising
e. random sampling	**5.** collection and analysis of information
f. cut	**6.** large stores or supplies
g. rates	**7.** remote-control, vehicle security locking system
h. sharply	**8.** an aspect which must be considered
i. survey	**9.** method or instrument
j. factor	**10.** to put one's argument too strongly; to exaggerate
k. sceptical	**11.** prices or charges for a certain quantity or amount
l. means	**12.** reduce
m. to take on board	**13.** to accept or adopt

❽ LISTENING • COMPREHENSION

 Listen to Part 3 of Julia Van der Merwe's presentation and answer the following questions.

a. '... it's not only the motorist who's *paying the price*'. What does Julia Van der Merwe mean by this?

b. What is the main theme of the presentation?

❾ TRANSFER

a. Practise presenting Diagram F.

b. Imagine you are Victor Decard or Robert Kerner. Make a brief oral summary of the presentation to management.

c. Management wish to consider the matter *in more detail*. They ask you for a written summary in 250–300 words.

⑩ READING

Read part of the text of a lecture on company finance (this is continued from Practice Section D). What is the meaning of the underlined words and expressions in brackets? Show that you know the meaning by using them in short sentences.

These problems can have far-reaching consequences.
   If a company cannot meet its <u>liabilities</u> when they <u>fall due</u>, it may try to <u>stall</u> creditors, who, if they *agree to* <u>postpone</u> payment of <u>sums due to</u> them, may <u>call</u> <u>for</u> a payment <u>deadline</u>. If the company fails to meet the deadline, creditors may then *take* legal *action* against the company *with regard to* the <u>overdue</u> payment. *In the last resort*, creditors can force the company to <u>close down</u>, so the company <u>ends up</u> <u>going out of business</u>.

⑪ TRANSFER

a. Prepare a presentation of your own, with graphics if necessary, using the Answer Key for Question 1 and the Tapescript as a guide, if you need to. The theme or topic can be of your own choice, for example presenting your company or one of its products or services. If you are working alone, record yourself on cassette and listen to yourself.

b. Write up to 250 words on how to avoid financial problems in business.

21 STUDY UNIT

Disagreement and Criticism

as far as (it) goes within certain limited incomplete or imperfect bounds

- Your argument seems logical, *as far as it goes*, but to be honest it does not <u>tackle</u> the real issues here.
- He's a good manager *as far as he goes*, an asset to the company, <u>up to a point</u>, but his obvious limitations <u>rule out</u> promotion.

at cross purposes having a difference of opinions, wishes or objectives, leading to confusion

- This is a complex matter, so let's set <u>up</u> our objectives before we start, <u>to make sure</u> we don't end up *at cross purposes*.
- You're thinking of a meeting next week? I was thinking of a meeting this week. I think we're talking *at cross purposes*.

to be beside the point to have no connection with what is being discussed; to be irrelevant

- The only important question is whether we <u>go ahead with</u> the project or not; anything else *is beside the point*.
- The finance manager's explanation that he authorised advance payments to suppliers <u>in order to</u> speed up delivery is *beside the point*, as what he did was against clear company policy.

(a) credibility gap the difference or distance between what one is able, or willing, to believe and what one is asked to believe; the extent of disbelief

- Statements made by the company earlier this year projecting healthy profits, are at variance with recent figures showing losses. This has created *a credibility gap*

between the company and its shareholders.

- The company's advertising claims about the qualities of its new product are not justified by its performance. This has <u>resulted in</u> *a credibility gap*, which the company will find hard to bridge <u>in the future</u>.
- You say that you took £10 from the petty cash box but £15 is missing. There's *a credibility gap* here, I'm afraid.

to have doubts about to have a negative or uncertain reaction or feeling about

- Due to the chairman's personal problems, I *have* serious *doubts* about his ability to <u>carry out</u> his functions.
- Although <u>at first sight</u> the proposal seemed a good one, we *had* some *doubts about* it and after <u>looking into</u> it we could see that it <u>was out of touch with</u> <u>reality</u>.
- 'I *have* my *doubts about* my future with the company.'
  'Really? I *have no doubts* <u>at all</u> about mine – I've just been promoted!'

(a) matter of opinion something not known or proved to be true or correct; something not believed by the speaker

- 'He's a good manager.'
  'That's *a matter of opinion*. I worked with him for two years and, <u>as a matter of fact</u>, that was the worst time in my career.'
- Whether one product is better than another is often *a matter of opinion* and one function of marketing is to shape people's opinion <u>in favour of</u> certain products.

- Although this idea is a good one in principle, as I think we're all agreed, it's still largely *a matter of opinion* whether it is workable in practice. In this meeting, I want to hear your views before any further decision is made.
- Remember, in this market survey we are interested in data, information and hard facts, not mere *matters of opinion*.

on the contrary in total contrast (to what has just been said), completely in opposition or reverse

- The board believed that the chairman would accept a large amount of money as an inducement to resign. *On the contrary*, however, he was unwilling even to consider it.
- 'Do you agree that the results are not as good as you had hoped?'
'*On the contrary*, they are at least as good, possibly better.'
- 'So, on the basis I've just described, you'd be prepared to accept our proposals?'
'*On the contrary*, I'm afraid further changes will have to be made before we can accept them as a whole.'
- The marketing director thinks we should expand into new markets now. The sales director, *on the contrary*, believes we should first explore existing markets in greater depth.

out of the question not a possibility [Also **there is no (not any) question of***]

- I'm afraid a further reduction in price is *out of the question*. We've already quoted you our best terms.
- Company managers tried to persuade creditors to postpone closing the company down, but they were told that this was *out of the question*.
- **There's no question of* our flight leaving tonight – the weather's too bad.

to pass the buck to try to avoid blame or responsibility by blaming someone or something else [Note: *buckpassing* can be used as a noun*] [Same as to shift the blame/responsibility and to put the blame on]

- You are in charge. You are responsible. If something goes wrong, there's no *passing the buck* – the buck stops with you.
- *This government accepts responsibility for its actions. It does not practise *buckpassing*. In answer to your criticism of our housing policy, however, I would like to make the point that slums are created by people, not governments.

to shift the blame (or **responsibility**) (**onto**) to try to transfer the weight or focus of blame or responsibility, misdirecting it from where it belongs, in order to avoid it [Also **to put the blame on***] [Same as to pass the buck]

- The sales department said that high interest rates gave rise to their poor results last year, but frankly I think they're just trying to *shift the responsibility*.
- The chairman *is shifting the blame* for the company's problems on to everyone but himself, when, in point of fact, everyone – and the chairman first and foremost – is to blame.
- *He is a bad manager, always *putting the blame* for his mistakes *on* other people.

to split hairs to disagree or argue over something unimportant [Note: *hairsplitting* can be used as a noun*]

- When we read the proposed changes to the contract, our first impression was that the other side were just *splitting hairs*. However, we quickly saw the light and realised the significance of the changes.

- *'On the whole, the other side's offer seems reasonable, although in my view we should hold out for a formal letter from them, admitting they were wrong, don't you agree?'
'On the contrary, I think you're just *hairsplitting* – let's just accept their offer.'
- 'I have a strong objection to the company accounts. I refer to the item:
'International Massage Services £3,750'. This creates a serious credibility gap between the company and its shareholders, such as myself, and I must insist on every penny being accounted for in full.'
'Thank you, this meeting will take note of your objection. However, clearly the word, 'massage' should read 'message'. In passing, may I remind you that the aim of the exercise at this meeting is to pass the company report and accounts, not *to split hairs* over an obvious misprint.'

up to a point partly; to some extent

- Yes, that's a good idea, and I agree *up to a point*, but there are some factors which you haven't taken into account.
- That the two governments have agreed to hold talks is good news, but only *up to a point*. It remains to be seen whether they compromise with one another over their differences or come to a dead end; it depends on both sides having an open mind.

(a) value judgement an opinion or decision based on personal feelings, subjectivity or wishful thinking and not on fact, knowledge, reason or objectivity

- In the early stages of both business and personal relationships, *value judgements* can keep people in the dark as to each other's true character and qualities. The end product depends on what occurs when they see the light.
- Breaking new ground in business is in the nature of a military exercise, in so far as progress is made by relying on hard facts and planning ahead in lieu of *value judgements* and trial and error.

22

STUDY UNIT

Conditions

as long as if the situation exists that, provided that, but only if [Also **so long as***]

- We are prepared to pay your asking price, *as long as* you can deliver on time.
- We are not going to make a profit *as long as* we continue employing too many people.
- *You can borrow the company car, *so long as* you realise you must refill the petrol tank and pay for any damage caused while the car is in your hands.

in case if it happens that; in order to be ready for

- We should arrive early for the meeting *in case* there are things to be done before it starts.
- Fire precautions state action to be taken *in case of* fire.
- *In case* we come up against any problems, we need to think out our game plan well in advance.

it (or **that**) **depends (on)** maybe; perhaps; (I) haven't decided yet, and anyway there could be conditions; it is very uncertain

- 'Can I go now?' I asked the customs officer.
  '*That depends*,' he replied, looking at the bottle of whisky in my hand. I gave him the bottle and he let me pass.
- 'Are you interested in our product?'
  '*It* all *depends*. First of all, what discount are you offering on your list price?'
- 'Have you decided about my salary increase?'
  'I think *that* rather *depends on* you,

doesn't it? Your performance so far certainly doesn't justify an increase.'

it (or **that**) **remains to be seen** it is not yet known or decided (whether)

- We are certainly interested in your proposal but *it remains to be seen* whether we can accept it or not.
- With the merger of the two companies just completed, the stock market reaction *remains to be seen*.
- 'When will the next dividend be declared?'
  '*That remains to be seen*. It depends largely on how soon the company is able to carry out its programme.'
- How many companies survive the recession *remains to be seen*.

on condition that (yes) but only if; (yes) but (in exchange) there is a special requirement that; on the understanding that

- You can use the company car *on condition that* you return it by tonight.
- We are prepared to pay your price *on condition that* you can guarantee delivery.
- Your estimate is acceptable, *on one condition – that* the work is finished within one month.
- Before we can start negotiating seriously, we need to find out *on what conditions* they are prepared to go ahead. On that basis, we can identify what are the areas of common ground, and what are matters for discussion.

23
STUDY UNIT

Logic and Reason

to account for to explain; to give a full or satisfactory answer for

- Price rises can *be accounted for* by increased demand or decreased availability of supply.
- The manager was reprimanded for failing to *account for* £250 he had spent on the company credit card.

common sense natural intelligence and understanding (not what is learned or taught) [Note: *common-sense* can also be used as an adjective*]

- *In this company, we're not a bunch of theorists and academics; we take a *common-sense* approach to business.
- *Common sense* suggests that regular exercise improves the quality of our daily lives, and our performance at work.

to hold water to pass or be able to pass testing or examination; to be sound

- Your explanation for the delay has been examined and I'm afraid it *doesn't hold water*.
- Arguments in support of the need for more staff *hold no water* at all.

to make sense to be logical; to have meaning; to be correct or capable of being understood

- For business travellers, *it makes sense* to travel in comfort. There's no point in flying economy class half way round the world to arrive exhausted for an important meeting.

- Your argument *would make* good *sense* in an ideal world, but it just doesn't hold water in reality.
- This letter is very confused, I can't *make* any *sense* of it at all.
- We are not making much progress at all in this discussion and I can't see that *it makes* any *sense* to continue. Let's break off now and come back and try again tomorrow.

to prove (the) case (or **point**) to show that an opinion or argument is correct or true

- The company is in trouble. Look at the rising overdraft and the falling sales figures – they *prove my point*.
- The government says the economic situation is improving. However, it's difficult to see how they can *prove their case* in the light of rising unemployment figures.

to tie in (with) to match; to correspond with; to fit (or to make or cause to fit); to corroborate; to coordinate

- It's difficult, but I can just *tie in* lunch between my morning and afternoon meetings.
- If we *tie in* our flight arrangements, you'll be arriving in Copenhagen from Paris just half an hour before I arrive from London.
- Our customer's failure to pay their invoice on time *tied in with* rumours that they were in financial difficulty.

Balancing Arguments

STUDY UNIT

either way This is the single or inevitable result whatever happens or is done (or whether it is true or not) [Also **one way or the other***]

- Whether we buy new equipment or employ new staff, *either way* we're spending money.
- If the government wins the election, interest rates will go up. If the opposition wins, social security payments will increase. So, we'll be worse off *either way*.
- *I don't seem to have much choice. The company wants to send me to England or the United States, so *one way or the other* I shall be working abroad.

for (and) against in agreement with and contrary to

- The government has carefully considered all arguments both *for and against* the new airport.
- Anyone with opinions *for or against* the proposal will have an opportunity to speak at the meeting.

on balance after considering all positive and negative features; all things considered; taking into account all factors for and against

- The board has given careful consideration to the arguments for and against introducing flexitime. *On balance*, we feel it would benefit the company.
- Although we have had good reason to criticise our UK agents a couple of times recently, I don't think we should change them, at least, not as yet because, *on balance*, they serve us well.

- Both machines are certainly excellent and it's hard to choose between them. However, *on balance*, perhaps the second one; it has a longer guarantee period.

on the one hand ... on the other (hand) in contrast

- There is a clear difference of opinion between us. We, *on the one hand*, want to maintain existing production levels with a reduced workforce, while you, *on the other*, want to increase both production and labour force levels.
- We need to improve our company image. *On the other hand*, we have to cut expenditure at the same time.
- We can certainly offer you £1,000 for your car. *On the other hand*, if you use it in part-exchange to buy a new car from us, we'll allow you £1,800.

(the) pros and cons the positive and negative aspects, features, factors or arguments

- At this meeting, we're going to look into *the pros and cons* of employing immigrant labour.
- Before taking any action on the draft proposals, we'd better get the legal department to advise us about its *pros and cons*.
- We're wasting time – while we're sitting here arguing *the pros and cons* of different types of office layout, our competitors are out there attacking our share of the market.
- After taking account of all *the pros and cons* of the matter, we feel on balance that it would be better not to go ahead.

to take into account (or **consideration**) to include as one of the important factors or things connected with a question, calculation or situation [Also **to take account of***]

- Product pricing policy should *take* factors such as marketing costs *into account*.
- Failure *to take into consideration* the views of the workforce could lead to a strike.
- *In international negotiations, cultural differences must *be taken account of*.

to weigh up to form an opinion or reach a conclusion by analysing and assessing information

- When making a presentation, it's a good idea *to weigh up* your audience beforehand, in order to judge their possible reaction.
- We *have* carefully *weighed up* your proposals and regretfully must decline your offer.
- The secretary quickly *weighed up* her new boss as a man who knew his job and treated his staff well.
- We can't make a snap decision on this matter – it needs *weighing up* carefully.

PRACTICE

A Plan for Negotiation

STORYLINE UPDATE

Boldmere PLC, a company specialising in the field of electronic security systems, wishes to market Auto Security Net (ASN), a vehicle anti-theft system on which it holds a provisional patent. Finance and marketing decisions (see memo and relevant graphics on page 12) led to Boldmere's proposals for finance to its bankers (see memo on page 29) and these were agreed. The board of directors, *consisting of* Jack Wagner (Chief Executive), Julia Van der Merwe (Marketing Director), Norman Buchan (Finance Director) and Narinder Dhillon (Technical Director), then agreed their marketing development strategy (see *game plan* on page 41).

An approach was made to the Department of Trade and Industry (DTI) for a code operator's licence, which ASN will require. Meanwhile, Narinder Dhillon made a series of technical demonstrations to police and motor insurers, whose cooperation is required *in order to* obtain a licence and to help market the product. However, the response received *made it clear* that a *full-scale dry run* of the system will be required before such cooperation can be given. The Boldmere board met to discuss the situation and this led to a tactical suggestion from Norman Buchan (see memo on page 63) which was adopted as part of the overall plan (see memo on page 64). *In accordance with* the company plan, Julia Van der Merwe and Narinder Dhillon made a series of presentations with follow-up technical demonstrations to the market.

However, it still remains to obtain the vital cooperation of Saturn, the telecommunications company, so that Boldmere can *tie* ASN *in* with Saturn's existing Greater London network.

STORYLINE

Motor manufacturers and accessory dealers, sceptical at first, began taking ASN seriously, *in principle*. However, a number of important points remained *to be smoothed out*. Moreover, it had now become clear that the *all-important* matter was to come to terms with Saturn. The initial breakfast meeting had *at least broken the ice*, with Saturn showing interest, and both sides went away *in order to* prepare for serious discussions. A formal meeting was arranged, to be attended by Jack Wagner and Norman Buchan *on behalf of* Boldmere, with Narinder Dhillon for technical back-up. Meanwhile, Boldmere's approach to the Department of Trade and Industry had *resulted in* an encouraging response, as you can see from their letter:

Department of Trade and
Industry
25 Westminster Lane
London W1 3NA
Tel: 081 956 3989

Boldmere plc
76 Blackstock Road
London N4 6QA

14 August 19--

Dear Sirs

TELECOMMUNICATIONS ACT 1984 CODE OPERATOR'S LICENCE

With regard to our discussions, I am able to inform you that a Code
Operator's Licence would not as a rule be withheld in the case of an
appropriate service which, in the view of this department, would
operate economically and fairly.

In addition, under the General Development Order 1988 planning
requirements can in general be satisfied by serving on the
appropriate local authority a letter giving twenty-one days'
notice of intent to instal equipment (the exception to the rule
being a fifty-six day notice where equipment is to be set up in a
conservation or green belt area).

These guidelines would hold true for a service on the lines set out
by yourselves and which suggest, on a first impression, that this may
be in the nature of development envisaged under the legislation.
However, in the light of the scope of the proposed scheme, the views
of relevant authorities, in particular the police, must be
ascertained and taken into consideration.

This letter is for information only and is without prejudice to the
powers and duties of this department in dealing with any formal
application for a Code Operator's Licence, which remains subject to
official approval until formal grant.

Yours faithfully

T. W. Mainspring

T. W. Mainspring
Department of Trade and Industry

❶ WARM-UP

In general, what preparations need to be made for a negotiation (such as the one between Boldmere and Saturn)?

❷ WORD STUDY

The following words and expressions are used in the storyline, the letter and in Question 3. What do they mean? Show you have understood their meaning by using them in short sentences.

a. to withhold
b. conservation/green belt area
c. to ascertain
d. approval
e. grant
f. to come to terms with
g. forthcoming
h. feedback
i. to commit oneself
j. measurably
k. at the end of the day
l. to buy an idea
m. to look at

n. manufacture under licence
o. to be with someone (two meanings)
p. low-key
q. to get the green light
r. on favourable terms
s. a phase
t. to put forward
u. outlay
v. to up
w. to cost
x. to take the line that
y. to work to someone's advantage
z. an agenda

STORYLINE

The Boldmere team now meet to discuss the current situation and tactics for the forthcoming meeting with Saturn.

---

❸ LISTENING • NOTE-TAKING • COMPREHENSION

a. Listen to the first part of the meeting and take notes about feedback from the market
(i) *In what respect* is this positive, *according to* Julia Van der Merwe?
(ii) what are the points that remain *to be ironed out*?
Also listen carefully to the discussion about the attitude of manufacturers and accessory dealers, so you can check this is *taken into account* in the Negotiating *game plan* on page 96.

b. Now listen to the second part of the meeting and take notes about the objectives and tactics for the forthcoming meeting with Saturn. You can then check to see if these are dealt with in the Negotiating *game plan*.

STORYLINE

After the Boldmere team meeting, and before the meeting with Saturn, Jack Wagner circulated the following memorandum. (This refers to Security Identification Numbers – see Practice Section C, Tapescript, Part 4.)

Boldmere plc

From: JW

To: NB/JM/(ND)

30 September

Re: ASN/Saturn Meeting Wednesday 05 October: Negotiating game plan

Background/update
Since my memo of 15 July, some progress has been made, that is:
- the DTI have given an off-the-record indication that licence to operate ASN will be granted, subject to the police being satisfied.
- our market has shown positive interest, but has made clear its insistence on being satisfied as to reliability of the system. As we know, there remain other matters to be sorted out (price/manufacture) but it is now crystal clear that everything depends on a successful dummy run, which in turn hinges on coming to terms with Saturn.

Game plan
The team will consist of myself, with NB and ND in attendance to deal with financial and technical matters. A brief technical run-through from ND to be followed by my setting out our proposals. That will be the proposed agenda – more than that could give away our game plan and we need to keep the other side in the dark up to a point. I shall deal with the main points, but if it goes according to plan NB will suggest the option at the appropriate time.

Aim
To negotiate terms in full for a phased option (including the right to set up a dry run) at a fixed fee to be set off against rental if we go ahead with full site-sharing. Phase 1 to be in respect of the Greater London area and the right to acquire Security Identification Numbers (SINs). Subsequent phases to depend on Saturn's own plans, but with a view to covering the UK and maybe abroad as well.

Our basic proposal

1. Pointing out our strengths: the system is patented and we have a positive response from the DTI, the police, the insurers and our market.
2. Stressing our status by making the point of our commitment to crime reduction.
3. Spotlighting the washback effect of improved buyer confidence in the motor market – and more cars could mean more car phones – the initial sweetener.
4. Introducing the idea that we are considering alternative ways of setting up the system and that one of these is operating in conjunction with an existing network, as long as it does not fall short of our requirements.
5. Confirming that we are confident that we have a viable system – the only question being, is theirs suitable for us to tie in with?
6. Focusing on the central issue – that we need to ascertain if their network is suitable and if, after we have tried it out, we decide that it is, then maybe we can consider further cooperation.

If this approach is correct, it will tackle in advance their anticipated probes for weakness on our part, reinforce our strengths and encourage them to see advantages to them of going ahead with us. The ball will then be in their court and they may then put the pressure on for full site-sharing in all phases in order to offset their own development costs. We will argue against that as being premature and then try to talk them round towards our aim. Once we have agreed in principle, the details of site-sharing can be thrashed out. In that respect it will be for them to take the initiative and we would need time out to consider our position.

❹ WORD STUDY

In the left-hand column are some words and expressions from Wagner's memorandum. From the list on the right find the word or expression closest in meaning.

a. update	**1.** obligation or promise
b. indication	**2.** to depend on
c. to sort out	**3.** a secondary or dependent result
d. to hinge on	**4.** on our side
e. a run-through	**5.** recent information
f. give away	**6.** reveal/disclose/betray
g. terms	**7.** a description/explanation
h. commitment	**8.** too soon or early
i. washback effect	**9.** to resolve
j. central issue	**10.** sign
k. probe	**11.** close enquiry or examination
l. on our part	**12.** the main point or question
m. premature	**13.** conditions of an agreement

❺ TRANSFER

Look again at Question 1 and check in the Answer Key. Compare this with your own notes and the Boldmere Negotiating *game plan*. Do you think the Boldmere team's preparations for the Saturn negotiation are *on the right lines*? If you are not sure, check the tapescript.

❻ TRANSFER • NEGOTIATING PRACTICE

Scenario A

Pietro Cardini is a Milan-based company involved in the manufacture of high-quality fashion clothing. Its trademark (PC) and design logo (a leopard) are famous worldwide. As a secondary business, it manufactures ready-to-wear garments and accessories of all kinds in Italy, while granting licences to a limited number of companies in other countries for the manufacture and distribution in those countries of similar products bearing the trademark/logo designs.

Pietro Cardini has recently *withdrawn* the licence of its sole United Kingdom licensee and now wishes to negotiate terms with another company for the manufacture and distribution in the UK of its ready-to-wear garments and accessories. The Pietro Cardini representative(s) will meet the representative(s) of one or more UK companies to negotiate terms.

With your partner(s), decide who is to represent Pietro Cardini and who is to represent Cutlass Fashions, a UK company seeking to obtain the licence. Pietro Cardini representatives read the negotiating brief on page 127. Cutlass Fashions representatives read the negotiating brief on page 130.

❼ FEEDBACK

When you have finished the negotiation, make a record of what was agreed. You should then tell one another how well (or badly) you think you (and they) did, and why.

Steps to Understanding

at first sight apparently at first; when seen for the first time [Also **at first glance***]

- *At first sight* the contract seemed normal. However, closer examination showed that it contained some unusual clauses.
- *The chairman, *at first glance*, seems just an ordinary person. It is only on getting to know him that you realise how unusual he, in fact, is.

at a glance by looking quickly

- The new product manager has arrived. You can see *at a glance* that he means business.
- Comparing these two diagrams, you can see *at a glance* that the one marked A shows a higher profit projection.
- I'm not sure if these figures are genuine. Maybe even an expert couldn't tell *at a glance*.

to be in the dark to not know; to be without information [Note: **to keep in the dark** means to deliberately make sure (someone) does not know*]

- It's no use asking me about the company's takeover plans – *I'm* as much *in the dark* as you are.
- 'Is there any news from the war zone?' 'I'm afraid not. There's strict military censorship and *we're* all very much *in the dark*.'
- We *are* still *in the dark* as to our competitors' intentions. However, we are looking into this urgently to try and throw some light on the matter.
- *We must *keep* our competitors *in the*

dark about our plans for as long as possible; the element of surprise is important.

to be in the picture to know; to have information [Note: **to put in the picture** means to give information*; **to keep in the picture** means to keep informed**]

- 'Do you know about the new import legislation in this country?' 'Yes, thank you, I'm fully *in the picture*.'
- Let's go over those points again, to make sure *you're completely in the picture*, before we go any further.
- 'Can you comment on the rumours that your company is in trouble?' 'I'm afraid I'm not *in the picture*. I don't work here, I'm just visiting.'
- *Until now, we've had to keep you in the dark about our plans. Today, however, we're going to *put you in the picture*.

- ****Thanks for the progress report. *Keep me in the picture*, will you, as to further developments.**

crystal clear clear beyond any doubt; without possibility of misunderstanding

- You seem to be in some doubt about your responsibilities, so let me make it *crystal clear* to you. Your job does not involve taking friends out to lunch on funds reserved for entertaining clients.

- The government statement made it *crystal clear* that public spending had to be reduced.

- Many of you here today have little knowledge about the new technology. My purpose this morning is to make its possibilities *crystal clear* to you.

- Every time I explain myself in *crystal clear* fashion, there's always someone who misunderstands.

(a) first impression first feelings, or initial reaction, caused as a result of a new experience or situation

- *First impressions* are not always reliable.

- My *first impression* was that his idea was not a good one. However, on second thoughts I could see the logic in it.

- As soon as we met, I thought, 'This man has a dishonest face.' That *first impression* was soon to be proved correct.

to leave open to delay a decision or conclusion until after further discussion or action

- Yes, I know there's a recession and cuts have to be made, but the question of cutting employees' bonuses should *be left open* until other possibilities have been looked into.

- They've made us a good offer but I think we should *leave it open* for the time being and see if we can get a better one.

on the face of it apparently (but not necessarily); as seems at first (and on the limited information available) to be true

- The contract looks OK *on the face of it* but we'll get the legal department to check it over in detail in any case.

- *On the face of it*, the company is doing well: profits are up, the order books are full, and so on. But in my opinion, this will not continue to hold good unless we start thinking ahead now.

- The proposal seems reasonable, at least *on the face of it*. But of course we need to look at it in depth.

- I can't think of any reason *on the face of it* why you shouldn't be promoted, although in the final analysis the decision will be made by the directors.

on second thoughts after giving the matter further consideration [Also **on reflection***]

- I liked the plan on paper. I've been looking into its possibilities in detail and now, *on second thoughts*, I like it even more than I did at first.

- At our meeting, we did express some interest in your product, that is true, but I'm afraid that, *on second thoughts*, we have decided that we have no need for it.

- *Yes, I know we agreed in principle, but *on* further *reflection*, I think there are some additional points to be discussed and agreed before we go any further.

on the surface upon looking at what can be seen from the outside, superficially

- *On the surface*, he is a charming, polite, well-educated man; his real personality, however, is very different.

- The meeting between the two Presidents was friendly, at least *on the surface* and in public, in spite of the differences between them.

(a) second opinion an opinion (usually expert) from someone not directly involved in a matter, where there is doubt or disagreement between those directly involved

- If we can't reach agreement on the value of the buildings, then we can ask for *a second opinion* from a professional valuer.

- At first, we weren't sure how to tackle the construction problem but, after taking *a second opinion* from soil experts, we were able to come to a decision.

to see the light to change from a wrong or mistaken belief, intention or course of action; to realise that one has been wrong

- Having worked hard all their lives, people reach retirement age and have time to think. Some of them then realise that their lives have been largely wasted. *Having seen the light*, they die from despair, bitterness and shame.
- At first, I couldn't understand what the presenter was aiming at, but bit by bit I began *to see the light*.
- His first career was in crime but after weighing up the risks and rewards, he *saw the light* and decided to become a politician instead.

to see reason to be persuaded by fair or logical argument

- Listen, you're good at your work, you follow the company rules, but this is the third time I've had to speak to you about your traffic violations in the company car. If you're not prepared or able to *see reason*, the company will have to think over your terms of employment.
- The logic of the lawyer's arguments was crystal clear, and yet the magistrates, who apparently enjoyed shared use of one brain cell, were unable to *see reason* and found his client guilty.

to sleep on it to take a short time (until the next day) to think something over before coming to a decision (informal)

- I've had second thoughts about our plans. Do you mind if I *sleep on it* and we can talk it over again tomorrow?
- You don't have to decide now. *Sleep on it* and let us know tomorrow.

to throw light on to give a reason or explanation for something which is not clear or apparent, to enable understanding [Also **to shed light on***]

- I can't understand these accounts at all. Would you have a look at them? Perhaps you can *throw* some *light on* them.
- Police investigations have so far failed *to throw* any *light on* the disappearance of the chairman, his secretary and £2m from the company bank account.
- *The process is not as complex as it may seem – this diagram may help *shed light on* it.

wise after the event to realise, after something has happened, what should (or should not) have been done before it happened

- Difficult and dangerous situations often produce experts, people who have not, in fact, taken part in these situations, but who are *wise after the event*.
- To make our marketing strategy work, it goes without saying that we need to keep ahead of our competitors. We do that by keeping them in the dark about our intentions, so in that way they only get *wise after the event*.

with hindsight with the help of an understanding of events which is only possible after they have happened

- The events of that period were so confused that only now, ten years later, *with* the wisdom of *hindsight*, can we look back and put the record straight.
- *With hindsight*, it is now possible to see the mistakes we made.

101

Summarising

all in all taking everything into account and weighing it up; summarising by comparing the positive and negative factors

- Although the company has had its problems over the last twelve months, *all in all* it has been a successful year.

- Weighing up all the important factors and allowing for the things which might go wrong, *all in all* we think we should go ahead with the idea.

(a) bare outline a short description; a few words giving only the most important facts [Also **(the) bare bones***]

- At this stage, I'm going to describe the process *in bare outline* only. My colleague will explain it in detail later.

- At this meeting, we'd like to give you our proposals *in bare outline*. If you agree in principle, we can then go on to discuss them in depth.

- *There isn't time to put you in the picture completely, so I'll just give you *the bare bones*.

in brief briefly; to summarise; in a word; in other words [Also **in short***]

- As we have seen, the facts are complex but, *in brief*, they can lead to only one conclusion.

- I'll give you all the details later but, *in brief*, the position is that we need to raise money fast.

- *So, *in short*, then, the situation is this: that our expansion scheme can continue, but in modified form.

in effect not in itself or directly, but in reality; in its actual meaning, effect or result; in practice; for all practical purposes

- With respect, although you've been speaking for twenty minutes, *in effect* you've told us nothing as yet.

- The change in the law, aimed at reducing unemployment, will *in effect* also increase public spending.

- The company's extravagant claims about the quality of its products *in effect* fell short of the truth.

in essence basically; fundamentally; as to only the central or most important facts or circumstances

- I agree with your idea *in essence*, although I have doubts about the way you propose to put it into practice.

- The two men's dislike for each other arose, *in essence*, from the fact that they had once been rivals for the same job.

- Our argument is based, *in essence*, on just two all-important factors: the need to reduce costs and the need to improve efficiency.

in a nutshell briefly; to summarise in a few words

- As we have seen, the company has a number of serious problems. *In a nutshell*, prompt and effective action must be taken, now, in order to avoid disaster.

- We have weighed up your proposals very carefully. Our decision, *in a nutshell*, is that we can only proceed on the basis you suggest on condition that you can guarantee no price increases for at least three years.

- The crux of the matter, *in a nutshell*, is that working conditions are so difficult that the workforce is insisting on a fifteen per cent pay increase.

in a word briefly; in short; to summarise [Same as in other words; in brief]

- I don't know why we ever employed him, *in a word* he's useless.

- *In a word*, our products are the best that money can buy.
- The graph tells the story; *in a word*, we've got problems.

the long and the short of it to summarise the main, basic or essential facts or result

- So, those, in brief are the options open to us. *The long and the short of it* is that, either way, we need greater production capacity and a more efficient delivery system.
- To give all the details would take too long. Anyway, *the long and the short of it* is that we have negotiated agreements to re-equip three power stations.

that is (to say) in other words; put differently

- Air consists of five elements: *that is to say*, oxygen, carbon dioxide, carbon monoxide, hydrogen and inert gases.
- Separation has a wind effect on passion: *that is*, a weak flame will go dead but a fire will switch to all systems go. (paraphrased from La Rochefoucauld: "Maxims")
- Our development policies are going nowhere fast: *that is*, they're forging ahead but they're not breaking any new ground.

27

STUDY UNIT

Steps to Compromise and Agreement

to agree on to reach or make agreement about

- The negotiators quickly *agreed on* two matters but could not *agree on* the others.

to agree to to accept

- I am afraid we cannot *agree to* your offer.

to agree with to have the same opinion as; to come to the same conclusion as

- The board *agreed with* the finance director's suggestion.
- The results of the experiment *did not agree with* the theory.

to be in line with to be in conformity or agreement with

- Although the manager's proposals were sound, they *were not in line with* company policy.
- Your ideas are very interesting, especially as *they're* very much *in line with* our own.

common ground a shared area of agreement or understanding; an overlap of aims or interests

- In a negotiation, it may be important to separate areas of agreement from those of disagreement: in a nutshell, to divide the *common ground* from the battle ground.
- There was enough *common ground* between the two teams of researchers to enable them to create an information pool.

to compromise (with) (over) to reach agreement by modifying or reducing one's stated objectives

- After lengthy negotiations, contract terms were finally agreed when the two

companies *compromised with* each other *over* prices and delivery schedules.
- The working relationship between the two managers broke down when they failed *to compromise over* shared use of office staff.

to do business (with) to trade or negotiate with a view to making money

- *We've been doing business with* that company for years and they've always paid on time; so what's gone wrong this time?
- Thank you for your time. We hope we can look forward to *doing business with* you in the future.
- We would like to *do business with* you, but if you're not able to play ball just a little on your pricing policy, it really isn't worth our while.

to draw up to arrange, prepare, draft or compose a written document

- Good, so, as you agree the terms, let's *draw up* your letter of employment now.
- The points agreed at this meeting can be faxed to our lawyers straight away so they can go ahead with *drawing up* the agreement.

give and take to make compromises or an exchange of concessions so that everyone gains or loses to the same extent

- We are ready to *give and take* in these discussions with a view to reaching overall agreement to our mutual advantage, and we hope that you will do so in the same spirit.
- All relationships, from marriage to business, call for an element of *give and take*.

- When setting up their objectives, negotiators need to know what they must have, what they should have and what they would like to have. In that way, they know how much they can *give and take*.

to go along with to share the same opinion as; to be or act in agreement with

- The company is happy *to go along with* your proposals.
- We're prepared *to go along with* you on price as long as delivery schedules are guaranteed.
- I'm afraid we can't *go along with* that suggestion at all.

in agreement (with) showing or having a shared opinion or conclusion

- *In agreement with* your recommendation, we have sold our shares in the company.
- I'm not altogether *in agreement with* these calculations.
- So, may I take it that we are *in agreement*, then?

in so far as to the degree, extent or amount that; in the sense that

- We will help you *in so far as* we can, but you must understand that our resources are limited.
- This company is different from others in the same field, *in so far as* it guarantees its products for up to five years, whereas the others do not.
- *In so far as* we are concerned, we cannot accept responsibility for loss of goods in transit and can only suggest that you contact your insurers.
- The two processes, while similar in their effect, differ *in so far as* one uses chemicals only and the other uses electricity as well.

to make (or **do**) **a deal (with)** to reach a business or commercial agreement

- I called the real estate agents about that house we saw last week but their clients already *made a deal* with someone else, so we're too late I'm afraid.
- She's a successful broker on the London Metal Exchange and *does deals* for a lot of clients.

- The new managers *made a deal with* senior staff of the company: in return for their cooperation in running the company, the senior staff would escape blame for company problems, the buck for which would be passed to a man known to be innocent.

to meet (someone) half way to compromise by a reduction in one's own demands, in return for a corresponding concession

- The company offered the workers a four per cent pay rise, in response to the union demand for ten per cent. Eventually, they *met half way* and agreed on seven per cent.
- If you're prepared *to meet us half way* on price, there's a better prospect of a repeat order.
- I'm afraid we have made our best offer, so we're unable *to meet you half way*, as you suggest.
- We entered into this negotiation in a spirit of compromise, but it is clear that you have no intention of *meeting us half way* on any of the issues.

off the record unofficially; not for the record; in confidence; not to be repeated, used or relied on in any way

- This is *off the record*, but one of the managers is leaving soon and you could be in line for his job.
- Speaking *off the record* – so, if there are any journalists here, don't quote me on this – the government now recognises that the new tax was not thought out carefully enough and it has caused some hardship. So, we may find some changes made, after the next election.
- Officially, we don't do business with certain countries, it's bad for our image in other parts of the world. But business is business and, *off the record* of course, we find ways of doing business with those countries, indirectly.

on (these) line(s) in this way; according to or by following this method, procedure, formula or pattern [Also **along (these) lines***]

- This year's conference will be *on the same lines* as before – a speech by the President, followed by a reception, and so on.

- The new managers will be running the company *on very different lines* from before.
- The new system is not working perfectly *as yet*, but we're *on the right lines*, I think.
- *So, that is how I suggest we approach the negotiations. If we go ahead *along those lines*, we have a better chance of getting results.
- *Your new employment contract will be *along the lines of* your last one, except for a salary increase.

on (these) terms in line with conditions or arrangements proposed or imposed

- This offer is not negotiable. Either you meet us *on our terms* or we can't go ahead *at all*.
- I'm afraid we're not prepared to do business *on your terms* – unless, on second thoughts, you are able to consider making some changes.
- From 1 June, all our prices will be increased by two per cent, in line with inflation. In addition, and in order to improve efficiency, weekly deliveries will be made in place of monthly ones. Please confirm you are prepared to continue doing business with us *on these terms*.
- *The terms on which* we agreed to sell you our products included a condition of payment within sixty days. We must remind you that payment on our last delivery is now overdue.
- That man has such a reputation for dishonesty that I don't think we can do business with him *on any terms* at all.
- Before we agree to lend you the money, you have to sign this loan agreement, which contains all our conditions. No changes can be made and we cannot go ahead *on any other terms*.
- We shall be happy to employ you again, *on the same terms* as before.

other things being equal only if other factors, conditions or circumstances (not directly being discussed) remain unchanged

- 'So, you are prepared to accept our offer?' '*Other things being equal*, we would be

prepared to accept, but the situation is changing all the time, as I'm sure you appreciate. So, we need a week or so to think it over before we decide.'
- *Other things being equal*, she always arrives on time. So, since she's late, there must be some good reason for it.

to see eye to eye (with) to agree, compromise or cooperate by first appreciating the other's thoughts and needs

- The kidnapper's voice came over the telephone: 'I'm sure that we can *see eye to eye* when I tell you that your chief executive is in a safe place and will be returned to you unharmed upon payment of DM1m in old notes.' The reply came that, as the chief executive was about to be dismissed, the company was not willing to do a deal.
- I think we're both trying to *see eye to eye with* each other, but we may be talking at cross purposes. Let's take time out for half an hour to think things over and then try again.

to settle (one's) differences to reach agreement or compromise on points or areas of disagreement in a discussion or relationship, so that only agreement remains

- By use of bribery, threats and promises, the company bidding for takeover caused disputes between the managers and shareholders, enabling it to launch a quick, successful bid before the others were able to *settle their differences* and put together a defence.
- Look, these are important customers, we can't afford to become involved in a dispute with them. We'll have to *settle our differences* with them somehow so we can carry on doing business.

to smooth out to remove problems or difficulties by discussion or action; to sort out; to put right [Also **to iron out***; **to straighten out*****]

- We're having some problems with the new machines but we're trying *to smooth them out*.
- *There are a few matters that need *ironing out* before we talk about your salary increase.

- **We have temporary financial problems but these should *be straightened out* within a few months.

to take note of to note, record or consider (when deciding or taking action) something which is indirectly connected, but which is not a factor to be taken into account

- The company *will take note of* an employee's preference not to be sent abroad, for family or other reasons. However, the interests of the company must take first place.
- The views of a large body of shareholders must not only *be taken note of*, they must also *be taken account of*.

to take (the) point to understand a reason, argument or point of view, but not necessarily to agree with it (also **to see the point**)

- 'We're never going to make any money if we go ahead on the lines you suggest. It's taking too much of a chance. It's like giving money away.'
  'I *take your point*. I know it's a long shot, but I'm convinced the scheme will pay its way.'
- 'We ought to hold out for our original asking price.'
  '*Point taken*, but surely that depends on whether the other side are able to pay it.'
- The unions are angry that our new policy was decided without their being consulted. You can *see their point*; after all, we did keep them in the dark, more or less until the last minute. I'm afraid we've got some softening up to do.

to think over to summarise mentally in order to decide one's present attitude or position with a view to future actions or decisions

- You don't have to come to a decision on our offer immediately – *think it over*.
- Our position needs *to be thought over* very carefully before we can think out a solution and take action on it.

to thrash out to solve or to overcome a problem (or to reach a solution) by frank discussion [informal]

- We've run up against a number of problems which need *to be thrashed out*, now, before any further steps can be taken.
- That's all for today. At our next meeting, *we'll thrash out* the matter of salary increases.

what if . . . ? suppose . . . ?

- *What if* we offered you a larger company car and a profit share in lieu of a salary increase? Would that be in line with your expectations?
- OK, so we try to persuade the President to retire. But *what if* the old fool doesn't see reason? *What if* he won't go of his own accord? We've then got to put pressure on him.

without prejudice (to) without reducing any existing right or withdrawing any existing claim, but in an effort to reach a compromise [legal English]

- We are prepared on this occasion to extend your time for payment, but you must remember that this concession is made *without prejudice* to our rights under the contract and must be regarded as an exception to the rule.
- We admit no legal liability in connection with your loss. However, in an effort to compromise with you over this dispute, we are prepared, *without prejudice*, to offer twenty-five per cent of your claim in full and final settlement.
- The empty factory can be used as a temporary dance studio, *without prejudice to* any future plans we may have to develop the site.
- Don't think that we're backing down in any way. Remember, these discussions are off the record and we're talking on a *without prejudice* basis.

Reasons for Decisions

STUDY UNIT **28**

the acid test the most effective and essential test of a quality

- Road trials of the new car will provide *the acid test* of its safety and reliability.
- *The acid test* of a top manager's ability is his performance under stress.
- *The acid test* of a product's saleability is whether the public buy it or not.

to base on to use as a basis; ground or system of reasoning

- Government policy *is based on* a balance between the freedom of the individual and the public good.
- The scientist's calculations *were based on* the results of his experiments.

in (or **under**) **the circumstances** in this particular situation; because of (special) conditions or influences

- We have found out about your criminal record. *In those circumstances*, we cannot employ you.

- Thank you for your fax of 23 June and we have taken note of your problems. *Under the circumstances*, we are prepared to allow a further seven days to carry out your contract obligations.

in that case because of that; that being so; since that is the reality of the situation

- The bank can make a larger loan over a longer period, but *in that case* it would be more expensive in terms of interest.
- So, all the terms between us are agreed. *In that case*, we can have the lawyers draw up the contract.
- We note you are not prepared to provide fresh components in place of the faulty ones you supplied. *In that case*, the contract between us is now terminated.
- Our competitors will probably reduce their prices in the near future. We should be forced to do the same *in that case*.

in the final analysis from a process of logic, it can ultimately be seen; when all the facts have been examined it is clear

- Many reasons are given for company failures but *in the final analysis* they are usually brought about by poor management.
- Our first impression of the new product was favourable, but *in the final analysis* its performance did not match up to its design.
- The pros and cons of this course of action must, of course, be discussed, but *in the final analysis* we have to make a decision either way.

in the light (of) according to; in relation to; when seen in relation to the following evidence; what is now clear (from) [Note: *in a new light* means in a different, fresh way (of seeing, knowing or understanding)*]

- Seen *in the light of* cold fact, many successful business people, pre-1900, were pirates and international criminals.
- *In the light of* the information we now have about that company's dealings, it is certainly clear that we should never have done business with them in the first place.
- *Her different approach to the problem enabled us to see it *in a new light*.

in view of taking into account; considering; because of

- *In view of* the fact that you have not replied to our letter of 19 July, we are taking immediate steps to recover the money due from you.
- *In view of* the success of the product, why was it withdrawn from the market?

on the basis (of) using something as a test or justification for reaching a conclusion; in accordance with a certain standard; in conformity with some requirement

- The new machine has been tested and, *on the basis of* the results, is satisfactory for its purpose.
- *On the basis of* recent market research, there seems to be a clear need for this kind of product.

- The shareholders accepted the takeover bid *on the basis of* two shares in the new company in exchange for every share in the old company.
- So, those are our proposals. If you are prepared to go ahead *on that basis*, please let us know.
- You say it would be cheaper to transfer production to a different location, but *on what basis*? We need to see hard facts and figures in support of your suggestion.

on the ground(s) of (or **that**) for the following reason(s); for the reason that; because of the fact or belief that [Note: generally used in the plural in normal written/spoken English] [Same as on the basis of]

- The young executive was dismissed *on the grounds of* his inefficiency and poor results.
- 'On what basis are you claiming that we have broken the contract?'
  '*On the grounds that* the quality of the products does not match their description.'
- The training department's budget has been cut by fifty per cent *on the grounds of* economy.
- Our decision not to renew the contract was based on policy *grounds* and we regret that no further details can be given.

G

PRACTICE

The Negotiation

Boldmere PLC, a company specialising in the field of electronic security systems, wishes to market Auto Security Net (ASN), a vehicle anti-theft system on which it holds a provisional patent. Finance and marketing decisions (see memo and relevant graphics on page 12) led to Boldmere's proposals for finance to its bankers (see memo on page 29) and these were agreed. The board of directors, *consisting of* Jack Wagner (Chief Executive), Julia Van der Merwe (Marketing Director), Norman Buchan (Finance Director) and Narinder Dhillon (Technical Director), then agreed their marketing development strategy (see *game plan* on page 41).

Narinder Dhillon made a series of technical demonstrations to police and motor insurers, whose cooperation is required *in order to* obtain a licence from the Department of Trade and Industry (DTI) and to help market the product. However, the response received *made it clear* that a *full-scale dry run* of the system will be required before such cooperation can be given. The Boldmere board met to discuss the situation and this led to a tactical suggestion from Norman Buchan (see memo on page 63) which was adopted as part of the overall plan (see memo on page 64). *In accordance* with the company plan, Julia Van der Merwe and Narinder Dhillon made a series of presentations with follow-up technical demonstrations to the market. *With regard to* the code operator's licence, which ASN will require, the Department of Trade and Industry has given positive indications.

However, it still remains to obtain the vital cooperation of Saturn, the telecommunications company, so that Boldmere can *tie* ASN *in* with Saturn's existing Greater London network. A meeting of the Boldmere board *resulted* in a negotiating game plan (page 96).

The Boldmere team arrive at Saturn's headquarters, where they meet Cynthia King, and Richard Fromm, Saturn's European Vice-President. After the introductions, and following Narinder Dhillon's technical run-through, Jack Wagner opens the negotiations.

110

❶ LISTENING · NOTE-TAKING

Before you listen to the first part of the negotiation meeting, look again at points 1–6 of Jack Wagner's basic proposal in his memorandum of 5 October on page 96.

Now listen to Part 1 of the meeting and check whether the six points are covered. Then answer the following questions.

a. How would you judge Saturn's reactions *so far*?
b. What do you think happens next? Who makes the next move? And what might that be?

❷ WORD STUDY

What is the meaning of the following words and expressions used in the opening part of the negotiation? Show that you understand the meaning by using them in short sentences.

a. I take it that
b. to raise a point
c. to come into it

d. to give a boost
e. that could be the case
f. to meet a requirement

❸ LISTENING · NOTE-TAKING · COMPREHENSION

Now listen to Part 2 of the negotiation, which follows on from where Part 1 left off. Take notes about what Saturn wants and why. Then answer the following questions.

a. How would you summarise the position adopted by Saturn?
b. What points does Norman Buchan stress as he suggests there could be a way to break the apparent *deadlock*?

❹ WORD STUDY

In the left-hand column, below, are some words and expressions used by the speakers in the meeting. From the list on the right, find the word or expression closest in meaning.

a. linking/link-up	**1.** to obtain or retrieve information
b. to access	**2.** capable of being used together
c. to overstep the mark	**3.** to come to terms
d. compatible	**4.** shared, common, reciprocal
e. all round	**5.** means of finding a solution
f. safeguards	**6.** comprehensive, in all respects
g. to sort something out	**7.** joining or connecting
h. the crux of the matter	**8.** the vital or central issue
i. mutual	**9.** to go beyond the correct limit
j. key	**10.** means of protection

❺ TRANSFER

Now look at the outline option proposals set out in Norman Buchan's memo of 13 July (Practice Section D). Practise presenting these to your partner, or into a cassette if you are working alone.

❻ LISTENING • NOTE-TAKING

 Listen to the final part of this stage of the negotiations. Take notes as you listen.

❼ TRANSFER

a. Imagine you are Cynthia King/Richard Fromm. Dictate a brief oral summary of the negotiation for the management team.
b. As Jack Wagner, write a short update memo for Julia Van der Merwe.

STORYLINE

A few days later Boldmere received rental information and a standard form of site-sharing agreement from Saturn. Shortly afterwards a draft Option Agreement prepared by Saturn's lawyers arrived. Although a number of points remained *to be straightened out*, the important matters between Boldmere and Saturn had been agreed *in principle*.

The next step would be to approach the market *with regard to* unit price, but first the insurers had to be persuaded to reduce premiums for vehicles fitted with ASN. *In turn*, this involved an approach to the police to obtain an estimate of the reduction in car thefts/increase in tracing stolen vehicles *resulting from* the introduction of ASN. This information would enable insurance company actuaries to calculate motor premium reductions.

However, none of this could be done until a *dry run had taken place* and *of course* this could not *be arranged for* until signing of the agreements. After several weeks more, the terms of the Option Agreement *had* finally *been thrashed out*. It is now Monday morning and Jack Wagner calls an urgent and immediate board meeting.

---

❽ LISTENING • COMPREHENSION

 Listen to the meeting and answer the questions below.

a. What is Jack Wagner's good news?
b. What do you think is in the newpaper article he mentions? (Turn to the last page of the Practice Section and read the article yourself.)

OPTION AGREEMENT: SITE-SHARING

THIS AGREEMENT ("the Agreement") is made and entered into on the day of   19– – by and between SATURN TELECOM INTERNATIONAL PLC with its principal place of business at 14 Canada Place Cabot Square London E14 8PQ (Facsimile: 71–637–6768/ Telex: 269169) (hereinafter called "Saturn") and BOLDMERE PLC with its principal place of business at 76 Blackstock Road Finsbury Park London N4 6QA (Facsimile: 81-704–2196/Telex: 432918) (hereinafter called "Boldmere")

1. RIGHTS GRANTED

1.1 Subject to the terms and conditions of this Agreement Saturn hereby grants to Boldmere an option to enter into a site-sharing agreement in the form annexed hereto such option to be valid and exercisable for a period of six months from the date of this Agreement and expiring at 2359 on the   day of   19

❾ TRANSFER

What would you advise the Boldmere team to do now?

❿ TRANSFER • NEGOTIATING PRACTICE

Scenario B

This is the second part of the negotiating excercise started in Practice Section F. A licensing agreement was negotiated between Pietro Cardini and Cutlass Fashions. However, after eighteen months it is clear that things are not running smoothly:

• UK sales are down, for reasons which are not entirely clear;

• there are signs of discord between the two companies: the licensee, Cutlass, is withholding payment of royalties due under the agreement, while the licensor, Cardini, has leaked to the press that it is negotiating a fresh agreement with an unnamed UK rival of Cutlass.

Representative(s) of Pietro Cardini and Cutlass Fashions have, however, agreed to meet to try to resolve their differences.

With your partner(s), decide who is to represent which company. Cardini representatives turn to page 131, Cutlass representatives to page 133.

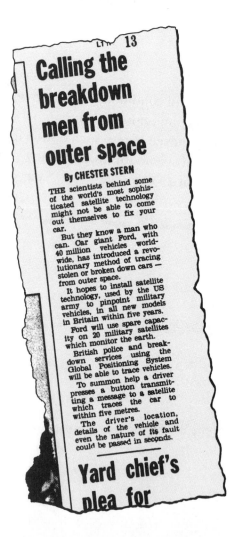

LTN 13

Calling the breakdown men from outer space

By CHESTER STERN

THE scientists behind some of the world's most sophisticated satellite technology might not be able to come out themselves to fix your car.

But they know a man who can. Car giant Ford, with 40 million vehicles worldwide, has introduced a revolutionary method of tracing stolen or broken down cars — from outer space.

It hopes to install satellite technology, used by the US army to pinpoint military vehicles, in all new models in Britain within five years.

Ford will use spare capacity on 20 military satellites which monitor the earth.

British police and breakdown services using the Global Positioning System will be able to trace vehicles.

To summon help a driver presses a button transmitting a message to a satellite which traces the car to within five metres.

The driver's location, details of the vehicle and even the nature of its fault could be passed in seconds.

Yard chief's plea for

Tapescript and Answer Key

Practice Section A

❷ WORD STUDY

a. **subsidiary** (of a company) with over fifty per cent of its capital stock owned by another company
b. **involved** concerned with; participating
c. **link** connection
d. **detection** discovering, finding out
e. **trace** to follow, discover, find
f. **vehicle** method of transport with wheels (cars, vans, lorries, motorbikes)
g. **provisional** temporary
h. **patent** government permission giving an inventor the sole permission to make, use and sell an invention
i. **sole** unique, the only one
j. **diversify** to vary products, operations
k. **prioritise** to list in order of importance
l. **resources** supplies, money, staff, skills *and so on* needed to achieve a task
m. **run out** to exhaust/become exhausted or expire
n. **Are you with me?** Do you follow my way of thinking or reasoning?
o. **the finished product** the complete, ready-to-sell product
p. **the crux of the matter** the vital or central issue or question *on* which all else *depends*
q. **in point of fact** the (perhaps surprising) reality is
r. **without more ado** immediately

❸ LISTENING • COMPREHENSION

Tapescript

Wagner: So that's agreed. Good. Right then, *last but not least*, can we *spotlight* our plans to diversify into Auto Security Net? *So far*, we've been dealing in ideas. But now the *all-important* question of patent protection has been *arranged for*. So this is *the moment of truth*, time to start talking in *hard facts. The aim of the exercise* now is *to make up our minds as to* exactly what *action we're going to take. That's to say*, we have to decide how to exploit our patent and, *in addition*, how we're going to finance the operation. And *in order to* do that, we need to *put together* a list of objectives with alternatives, and then prioritise. Julia?

Van der Merwe: Yes, thank you, Jack. Well, *in my opinion*, our *game plan* should be this: we *go for* world markets *straight away*. We've got provisional patent protection worldwide, so, *first and foremost* we should *take the initiative*. That gives us time *to go ahead* and get into world markets *at once*, ahead of competition . . . .

Buchan: Hum! That *makes sense* up *to a point*, but I can see a serious *drawback* there. You see, *the fact of the matter is that* our resources *in terms of* both production and finance are limited. *What's more*, the product looks good *on paper*, but *as yet* it hasn't been tested on the market. You see, *I take the view that* we should first promote the system on the domestic market. That must *take first place*. You see, if we *run up against* any problems we can *smooth them out* on our home territory, before *taking steps to* tackle the overseas market. But *above all* our marketing must be realistic, not only *as such, in its own right*, but also *in terms of* our financial capability, the two go *hand in hand*. If we market worldwide and things start *to go wrong*, we just won't be able *to cope with* it. We'd be *running far too great a risk*, and I don't like to think of *the price we'd have to pay* if it does *go wrong*. No, *in the short term* we should *focus on setting up* on the home market. *Better to be safe than sorry.*

Van der Merwe: Yes, I *take your point*, and it's a good one, *as far as it goes*. But *what if* we do as you suggest and then find that our patent protection runs out and we can't get a full patent worldwide? The answer to that one is *crystal clear*. Our competitors get into world markets and we have to *make do with* what's left: a smaller share of the market or none *at all*. And all because we didn't *go for it in time*. No, we have to *take a long-term view* and *aim at* world markets *from the outset*.

Wagner: Can I stop you there? I think we're already getting into an either/or situation. And *it's not as simple as that*. You've both *made a good point*. But I think, *in fact*, you may be talking *at cross purposes*, because the one possibility doesn't have to *rule out* the other. I'm being mysterious *on purpose*. I can explain why, and I'll *come to the point in a moment*. But let's *take time out* for coffee first, it's getting late, we need it and I need a few minutes to collect my thoughts.

Answers to Comprehension Questions

a. To decide how to exploit the patent and *in addition* how to finance the operation.
b. To get into world markets *straight away*.
c. So they can take advantage of provisional patent protection.
d. He sees problems.
e. Because of production/financial limitations and as the product has not yet been tested on the market.
f. Promote the system on the domestic market.
g. Because marketing worldwide is too risky.
h. No.

❹ WORD STUDY
a. 8.; b. 2.; c. 4.; d. 7.; e. 3.; f. 5.; g. 1.; h. 6.

❻ WORD STUDY
a. 6.; b. 5.; c. 12.; d. 9.; e. 11.; f. 13.; g. 10.; h. 7.; i. 3.; j. 8.; k. 2.; l. 1.; m. 4.

❼ LISTENING • NOTE-TAKING
Tapescript
Wagner: OK, to *get down to business* again. As I was saying, I *go along with* you both. And that, *in a nutshell*, is the crux of the matter. *In short*, rather than seeing each solution *in contrast to* the other, it's *a matter of* finding a solution where both your ideas *meet each other half way*. Are you with me *so far*?

Van der Merwe: You mean you're going to try and *talk us round*?

Wagner: Well, I hope I can manage to do that, but *that remains to be seen*.

Buchan: At the moment, I don't see how, but OK, I'm listening.

Van der Merwe: Me too.

Wagner: OK, well, as a matter of fact we don't have the resources, *in the shape of* either finance or production capability to market worldwide *of our own accord*. That's *on the one hand*. And *in reality* we do need to market the system here at home so that if it *falls short of* expectations in any way, we can *get to the bottom of* the problem here. But, as Julia said, we have to get into world markets before our provisional patent protection runs out. Remember, *above all*, we have to *get our priorities right*. And those are the priorities. So, it's not *a question of* choosing between them, the choice has already been made for us.

Buchan: But I still don't see how . . .

Wagner: Well, the way I see it is this. We get the product on to the home market without more ado. We can then show it to possible overseas contacts so they can see how it works . . .

Van der Merwe: So we use the system in operation here to attract foreign buyers?

Buchan: Or possible agents or distributors?

Wagner: Yes, or even possible joint venture partners. Anyway, *in that respect*, as *a means to an end* while the system is *in the course of* being tested.

Buchan: But surely there are dangers? If something *goes out of action*, or the system *breaks down* completely . . .?

Wagner: We'll just have *to take that chance*, I'm afraid. *In any case*, we'll be able to do a few *dummy runs* before anyone sees the system in operation, and it can be *checked over to make sure* it's in good working order. But it is *a risk we'll have to take*. Also, look at it this way, by *putting the pressure on* ourselves, we're more likely to have any problems *smoothed out* quickly, so the finished product can be promoted *ahead of schedule*.

Buchan: Mm . . . But I still think that's *taking a chance*. And I don't think we should just make *a snap decision* about it, either . . .

Van der Merwe: Yes, we need to *think it out* carefully. I like the idea *in principle*, though.

Wagner: OK, *point taken*, but we have to *make our minds up in the near future*. Let's *thrash it* *out* further. Let me see, can I take it you're both free on Monday at the same time?

Van der Merwe: Uh-huh, that's fine.

Buchan: Hang on, just let me check, yes, yes that's fine.

Wagner: Me too. Right, so let's *think it over in the meantime,* shall we, and try again on Monday. I'll *look forward to* that. Look at the time, ten o'clock, *in future* we'll really have to try and start *on time* and *zero in on* the main business *right away.* We're going to feel like zombies in the morning.

❽ WORD STUDY
a. 3.; **b.** 6.; **c.** 9.; **d.** 1.; **e.** 12.; **f.** 11.; **g.** 4.; **h.** 5.; **i.** 2.; **j.** 8.; **k.** 10.; **l.** 7.

❾ COMPREHENSION
a. He *agrees with* both solutions.
b. No, he thinks a compromise solution is best.
c. Boldmere does not have the production/financial resources to market worldwide *of its own accord* and the system needs testing on the home market first, but the company must get into world markets before its provisional patent runs out.
d. Get the system on to the home market as soon as possible and show it in operation to overseas contacts.
e. To resolve the problem at the next meeting and *to think it over in the meantime.*

⓬ TRANSFER
a. stems from/has an impact on/gives rise to/arise from/bring about/trigger off/results in

Practice Section B

❶ WARM-UP
a. • finance from the company's own resources: capital or reserves
• venture capital, in the case of high-growth companies or high-risk products
• the stock exchange (only available to public companies) or the unlisted securities market
• clearing or merchant banks
b. *In essence,* the soundness of the proposal, ability to repay and the value and type of security offered

❹ WORD STUDY
a. **credit** money lent or made available *in excess of* money deposited
b. **glad** pleased/happy
c. **to look at** to consider; study *in detail* and *think over*
d. **policy** a system of operation
e. **prudence pays** it *makes sense to take care*
f. **a bad credit record** a past history of failing to repay loans or debts
g. **sources** points or places from which something originates or may be obtained
h. **factors** important points or elements
i. **proposal** something (a plan, etc.) put forward for consideration
j. **combating** fighting (against)
k. **device** machine, tool or apparatus used for a specific task
l. **fitted** attached to
m. **linked** connected
n. **transceiver** combined transmitter/receiver
o. **sites** places
p. **elements** essential parts of a whole
q. **enable** to make possible
r. **potential** possible but not proven capability
s. **field trials** tests to show performance/efficiency
t. **projection** a prediction *based on* known facts
u. **item** thing or detail
v. **quoted** stated

❺ WORD STUDY
a. 4.; **b.** 1.; **c.** 7.; **d.** 2.; **e.** 5.; **f.** 3.; **g.** 6.

❻ LISTENING • NOTE-TAKING
Tapescript
David Evans: That *puts me clearly in the picture*, Mr Wagner, your company certainly seems *to be breaking new ground*, I hope it works for you. Anyway, *on the face of it*, this proposal seems to be in order – *at least in general terms.* So, can we *refer to* your financial requirements *as such*?

Wagner: Yes, as you know the total we need is one point four million, that's *in all*, but the company can raise eight hundred thousand *of its own accord*. So, the borrowing requirement *as such* is six hundred thousand ...

David Evans: May I stop you there a moment? You say the company can raise eight hundred thousand *of its own accord*, does that mean in *its own right* or by issuing shares or bonds?

Wagner: Uh-huh. That's all from reserves *for the time being*, though if we *get past first base* we'll be looking at a substantial share issue. Would you be able to handle things *on our behalf in that connection* if it comes to it?

David Evans: We could certainly *look into* that. Anyway, *in itself*, your current proposal need be *no problem in so far as* there is no borrowing from other sources, but I'll need to see more details. *With regard to* the borrowing, what proportion do you see *in the nature of* a loan, and how much as overdraft?

Wagner: We're speaking *in terms of* a four hundred and fifty thousand loan and a hundred and fifty thousand *in the shape of* an overdraft. *According to* our finance department, that's the best way.

David Evans: Mm, OK. Just *in passing, in respect of* any share issue, what exactly would that *consist of*, do you know?

Wagner: Our finance department would need to work on that one.

David Evans: But any share issue would be *in accordance with* the company statutes?

Wagner: Yes, *of course*.

David Evans: Yes. Now, *as to* your parent company in the States . . .

Wagner: Intersystems Inc. Yes, as you know, we operate independently and they've *got nothing to do with* the financing of this operation, although they did *set us up to start with, by the way* they took a first mortgage on our premises to secure their investment. And also, as you know, I'm an executive Vice-President of Intersystems. But we'd be working *hand in hand* with them on the marketing side over there. And *of course* they're *in touch with* developments.

David Evans: Uh-huh. Right, so what term do you have in mind?

Wagner: Well, looking at the borrowing *in aggregate*, we see it *in the nature of medium-term* finance. But that's *averaging it out. In practical terms* the overdraft would be *shorter term*, just to tide us over *in case* we don't meet our budget. Two years *at the outside*. The loan element *is another matter*. If we *come up against* serious problems, or even *a dead end* with this scheme, then the bottom line is that that's going to be dead money, I'm afraid. *In effect*, that's the extent of the *risk we're taking*. But a *worthwhile price to*

pay, *in view of* the potential profits if we *pull it off*. So *in that respect*, the loan *that is*, we'd like four to five years.

David Evans: That sounds reasonable, Mr. Wagner. Now, what form of security were you thinking of offering?

❼ WORD STUDY
a. **to raise money** to obtain money
b. **a borrowing** customer's loan from bank
c. **shares** basic parts of a company's capital stock
d. **bonds** a certificate of debt issued *in order to* raise money
e. **reserves** cash held to meet future expenses
f. **substantial** large
g. **issue** making (shares) available to buy
h. **an overdraft** money withdrawn *in excess of* a credit balance on a bank account
i. **company statutes** (in England, *Memorandum & Articles of Association*) document regulating a company's internal and external dealings
j. **parent company** company having *in excess of* fifty per cent of the stock of a subsidiary
k. **term** (repayment) period
l. **dead money** money spent *in vain*
m. **security** an asset that a lender can claim *in case* a borrower fails to repay a loan
n. **sound** safe, realistic, reasonable and logical
o. **a facility** bank loan for a specific purpose
p. **second mortgage** a document giving security *in the shape of* land or buildings but which is second in priority to an earlier (first) mortgage
q. **premises** land and buildings where a business operates
r. **a debenture** a bond at fixed interest
s. **undertaking** all a company's business and assets

❿ WORD STUDY
a. 4.; b. 5.; c. 6.; d. 1.; e. 3.; f. 2.

⓫ WORD STUDY
a. **terms** conditions for doing business
b. **formalities** requirements
c. **board** group of people responsible for managing a company
d. **to fall within** to be included in
e. **to go public** to convert from private to public company
f. **company mission** in marketing, a company's general task or aim

g. **market** trading/selling opportunities offered by a particular group of people

h. **trade** the people and practices of a particular industry/business

i. **features** aspects of a product

j. **benefits** advantages that a product provides to the consumer

k. **approval** formal agreement/favourable opinion

l. **licence** formal/official permission to do something

m. **network** interconnected group or system

n. **compatible** capable of being used *in conjunction*, without being adapted or modified

o. **facilities** means or equipment making it easier *to carry out* some task or function

p. **to access** to approach, enter and make use of something

⑫ LISTENING • NOTE-TAKING • COMPREHENSION

Tapescript

Wagner: Julia, you were *looking into* some possibilities. What have you *come up with*?

Van der Merwe: Yes, a couple of points on the marketing side. First of all I went back to basics. *In marketing terms*, the company mission is to fight crime. And our number one business target is crime prevention. We have to *base* our marketing strategy *on* that.

Wagner: Okay, and the second point?

Van der Merwe: Yes, the second is the *impact* that the recession is *having on* our market, *that is*, the motor trade, and somehow we have to *get it across* to the market that this is a *worthwhile* product, something the market needs in spite of the recession.

Wagner: That *makes sense*.

Van der Merwe: Exactly, a *common-sense* approach is what we need. So what I have in mind is this. We have to take the line that this product is not a luxury feature, like a car stereo, for example, but that *in itself* it has real benefits. That's *the first step*. But, *in order to* do that, we have to produce some *hard facts to prove our point*. Then we have to see to it that the market *takes the point* when we do a *try-out* of the system. Then maybe we start *opening a few doors*.

Wagner: Uh-huh, so . . .?

Van der Merwe: But I haven't *come up with* any more answers *as yet*.

Wagner: Okay, but what you're saying sounds good *so far*. Narinder, any ideas?

Dhillon: Well, *of course* we need to get DTI approval.

Van der Merwe: I didn't catch that, who . . .?

Dhillon: DTI, that's the Department of Trade and Industry, the government, *in effect* . . .

Van der Merwe: Oh, right, yeah.

Dhillon: Yes, because of the way ASN operates, we have to get DTI permission for what's called a code operator's licence. For example, look at Saturn, the mobile phone company. Their system is much the same as ours *in terms of* electronics. They had to get a licence.

Wagner: Saturn, they operate in London, don't they?

Dhillon: Well, they're planning a whole network, all over, but *for the time being* they've got the whole of Greater London covered.

Van der Merwe: Uh-huh!

Dhillon: But anyway, *to come to the point*. I've spent the best part of the last few weeks *looking into* it. And *in all probability* their system and ours would be compatible. And that means that if we can talk them into letting us share their sites and facilities, we could get *set up* quicker and cheaper than we'd *allowed for*.

Wagner: Fantastic.

Van der Merwe: Brilliant, so you're more than just a handsome face, then?

Dhillon: Stop it Julia! You'll have me blushing *in a moment*! Anyway, *what's more*, the police could access the system easily enough to trace any stolen cars. But as I said, we need DTI permission, even before we do a *dummy run*.

Van der Merwe: Mm, that gives me an idea.

Wagner: Go on, *don't keep us in the dark*, Julia.

Van der Merwe: Mm, just something *taking shape*, the police, stolen cars, insurance companies . . .

Answers to Comprehension Questions

b. Firstly, marketing strategy must be *based on* the company mission – to fight crime – and on its prime business target – crime prevention. Secondly, *in view of* the recession, the market has to be persuaded that ASN is a real benefit *in marketing terms*, not simply a luxury feature. Thirdly, *in order to* achieve this, statistics will be needed.

c. *That remains to be seen.*
d. 1. DTI permission will be needed for a code operator's licence. 2. If, as seems probable, ASN is compatible with the existing Saturn telecom system, operating *in conjunction* could save time and money.
e. *That remains to be seen.*

Practice Section C

❶ WARM-UP
Suggestions for a technical demonstration – consider the same factors as you would *take into account* when making a presentation, *that is to say* the following questions:
Who? What kind of audience, are they likely to be receptive or hostile, what is their level of technical knowledge?
What? Exactly what point do you want to *get across*?
Where? Location and facilities available will determine your approach.
Why? Your aim.
How? Your method of presentation, for example, *in view of* probable time limitations, how best to *make an impact*, what visuals to use, *and so on.*

❷ WORD STUDY
a. 6.; b. 8.; c. 1.; d. 9.; e. 2.; f. 7.; g. 3.; h. 10.; i. 4.; j. 5.

❹ WORD STUDY
a. on behalf of
b. in particular
c. get down to business
d. straight away
e. the aim of the exercise is
f. the long and the short of it is
g. in our opinion
h. a breakthrough
i. it's as simple as that
j. the facts will speak for themselves

❺ LISTENING
Tapescript Part 1
Dhillon: *On behalf* of my company, I'd like to welcome you to this demonstration. *In particular*, may I thank you for your time, which I know is valuable to you, so I propose to *get down to business straight away. The aim* of *the exercise* is to demonstrate a new product developed and

patented by my company. We call this product Auto Security Net, or ASN for short, and the *long and the short of it is* that this product, *in our opinion*, is a *breakthrough* in auto theft prevention, *it's as simple as that.* But we are confident that *the facts will speak for themselves.*

❻ WORD STUDY
a. 5.; b. 9.; c. 12.; d. 1.; e. 15.; f. 2.; g. 6.; h. 14.; i. 3.; j. 4.; k. 7.; l. 13.; m. 11.; n. 8.; o. 10.

❼ LISTENING • NOTE-TAKING • COMPREHENSION
Tapescript Part 2
Dhillon: Let me *put you in the picture.* We have here a car not fitted with a car alarm. The owner left it outside here about half an hour *or so* ago. *In a moment* you will see someone, not the owner, enter the car and drive it away. *Of course* this person is very happy to find no burglar alarm fitted, so he thinks he can drive it away *at will.* Here he comes. And there he goes. *In short*, the owner loses his car. *In addition*, police resources are spent trying to locate it. Even if they are lucky enough to do that, *in all probability* they won't catch the thief, in spite of all their running *back and forth. What's more*, the insurance company *stands to* make a payout *amounting to* several thousand pounds. This incident is typical of hundreds *on average taking place* every day in our city streets. Those are *the hard facts*, as we all know.

As we have seen, the car has been stolen. *No problem! At least* so the thief believes. But *on the contrary*, however, *in fact* he will soon be *looking forward to* a period as a guest of Her Majesty's Government in one of the special hotels provided for people like him. But, he's *in the dark* about that at the moment, as perhaps you are, too. So, let me *come to the point.* This car, my car, is fitted with ASN.

Answers to Comprehension Questions
b. To make an impression on the minds of the audience.
c. prisons (an example of English humour)

❽ WORD STUDY
a. consists of;
b. in effect;
c. rely on;
d. triggers off;
e. to spotlight;
f. to do with;
g. that is to say;
h. allowing for;
i. more or less;
j. and so on;

k. in turn;
l. in all;
m. at all;
n. in brief;
o. by the way;
p. paying the penalty.

❾ LISTENING

Tapescript Part 3

Dhillon: ASN *consists of* an electronic device fitted to the alternator, or generator as some people call it, and this, *in effect*, is powered by the engine so it doesn't have to *rely on* stored power or a power source vulnerable to defect or lack of use, such as a battery. This device *triggers off* a signal when the engine is running. There are two important factors *to spotlight* about this signal. First, each signal has its own unique digital code. This is *to do with* the make, model, colour and registration mark of the vehicle. Second, the signal itself is digital, *that is to say*, it is computer-controlled, computer-generated and interpreted, when necessary, thus *allowing for* greatly increased capacity within the system at any given time.

Anyway, when transmitting, the signal covers a radius of one kilometre *more or less* and is picked up by one or more transceiver sites already in place and arranged as a network of cells. Each cell interacts with its neighbour *and so on* and *in turn* the entire network is coordinated by a series of roughly ten switch centres *in all* which cover the whole of the Greater London area.

As I said, the signal is only interpreted *at all* when needed, *that is*, when the vehicle is stolen. The police will have access to the switch centres. So, all I have to do is call the police, the police then access the switch centre and this indicates the position of the vehicle to within a thousand square metres. *By the way*, this is a silent signal, so the thief has no idea that he will soon be *paying the penalty* for his actions.

❿ LISTENING • NOTE-TAKING • COMPREHENSION

Tapescript Part 4

Dhillon: That's the system *in bare outline*. Now, before I *zero in on the ins and outs of* it, are there any questions?

Joe Davis: Uh, yeah, you said the system is digital; why not analogue?

Dhillon: Hmm. Good question, that. Well, as you know the analogue system differs from the digital *in one all-important respect*: it *relies on* air waves. Now there is already *a good deal* of overcrowding on the air waves and that means limited capacity, so, *by the same token* an analogue system would need a separate power source. *To put it simply*, if we use an analogue system, as the existing mobile telephone networks use, we limit the number of vehicles the system can be fitted to, whereas the digital system has almost unlimited capacity. *What's more*, the system could not be *relied on* in the same way as the digital system can. Does that answer your question?

Joe Davis: Yeah.

Dhillon: Right. Ah, yes?

Evelyn George: So you're saying that with the digital system there'd be no limit to the number of vehicles that could be fitted with, uhh, ANS?

Dhillon: ASN, yes, that's right. *In fact*, that brings me to my next point. It's *worth mentioning* that we could *set this system up of our own accord*. But the best way to operate is to *tie in with* an existing telecommunications operator. Telecom systems are moving towards a system known as Personal Communications Network, or PCN for short. This uses digital technology to handle computer-controlled signals. So, we shall be operating *in conjunction with* one of these. *In fact* we're currently *in touch with* them to discuss terms. And their system, because it's digital, provides an unlimited number of security identification numbers, or SINs for short, for users of our system. So the system could operate *on a very large scale*.

Evelyn George: Yeah, yeah, but surely you'll need government permission for all this? And there's no guarantee you'll get it *for sure*, is there? And it's *a safe bet* that even if you do it'll take years. So doesn't that just *rule out* your idea?

Dhillon: *Point taken. In fact* various permissions and licences will be needed from various government departments, *in particular* the DTI, and we're *taking steps* on that right now. We need to show that we're working *hand in hand* with the police and insurance companies *in order to* get permission *in principle*, then we can *go ahead*, even though it could take several years *to arrange for* licences and permissions *in full*.

Evelyn George: You mentioned one telecommunications company. Do they cover the whole country?

Dhillon: *As yet*, no they don't. *For the time being* they operate only within the M25 London orbital motorway area, *to be exact*. However, *depending on* the outcome of our negotiations, we would expand our system *in conjunction with* theirs *in the future*. And *in any case* they do intend to have the country *as a whole* covered *in the medium term*, ten to fifteen years *at the outside*.

Joe Davis: So *at most* you could provide a service for the London area only?

Dhillon: *At the outset*, yes. But, *allowing for* the fact that the number of vehicles in London *averages out at* two million a day and vehicle thefts are running at around 250,000 a year *in aggregate*, *give or take* a few hundred *either way*, that's enough to put the system to *the acid test*.

Joe Davis: You say you're *breaking new ground*. But there are already anti-theft devices *in all shapes and sizes* on the market and almost *every other* new car is fitted with one. So why use your system *in lieu of* the others?

Dhillon: With car thefts *in excess of* five hundred a day, I'm *taken aback* at the question. But *in any case* we're not suggesting that the other systems are *duds*. What we do suggest is that our system offers clear advantages, *ranging from* improved customer protection at a lower cost *in real terms*, *to* prospects of higher recovery and arrest and conviction rates. *In the final analysis* the consumer is the decider and we believe that many consumers will think it *worthwhile* to use our system either *in place of* other systems or simply to back them up.

Answers to Comprehension Questions

b. That brings me to my next point.
c. Because analogue *relies on* air waves which are already overcrowded, it has limited capacity and requires a separate power source. So the number of vehicles which could be fitted with ASN would be limited if the analogue system was used. And *by the same token* it would not be as reliable as the digital system. *On the other hand*, ASN requires no separate power source and there would be no limit to the number of vehicles which could be fitted with it.
d. It uses digital technology to handle computer-controlled signals.
e. Permission *in principle* is enough *to go ahead*.
f. He says it will *at the outset*.

g. Because ASN offers clear advantages, *ranging from* improved customer protection at lower cost *in real terms*, *to* prospects of higher recovery and arrest and conviction rates. ASN may be used either as an alternative to other systems or to back them up.

Practice Section D

❷ WORD STUDY

a. **viable** capable of development
b. **indicated** stated, implied, *pointed out*, showed
c. **willing** ready, with a positive or favourable attitude
d. **assist** help
e. **staff** group of people employed by company/organisation
f. **appropriate** (*adjective*) right or suitable
g. **endorse** give or indicate approval or support
h. **contrary to the public interest** against the good order or security of the community or the state
i. **legitimate** *in accordance with* the law
j. **means** way or method
k. **detection** discovery
l. **viewed favourably** regarded in a positive way or with good opinion
m. **proceed** *go ahead*, continue
n. **device** machine, tool or apparatus used for a specific purpose or task
o. **promising** showing cause for belief in future success
p. **effectiveness** production of positive result
q. **evidence** data *on* which *to base* possible proof
r. **theft** stealing
s. **claim** demand (eg, for payment)
t. **appreciate** *to take into account* fully
u. **actuary** statistician employed by insurance company to calculate risks, policy premiums and dividends
v. **assessing** calculating value or amount, evaluating
w. **premium** amount paid for an insurance policy
x. **reserve final judgement** delay final decision until all evidence is available

y. members people belonging to or having an interest in an organisation (eg, shareholders)

z. policyholders holders of documents containing insurance contracts

❸ WORD STUDY

a. The company has made a profits projection, but the outcome will not be known until the year-end balance sheet is prepared.

b. We obtained provisional agreement for site-sharing with the TV company.

c. It is a tough job, but we can handle it.

d. They are caught up in a loveless marriage.

e. They thought up a concrete scheme to promote the product to the target market.

f. In an effort to boost sales, motor manufacturers are to offer customers a package, including discounts of up to thirty per cent on accessories.

❺ WORD STUDY

a. 4.; **b.** 5.; **c.** 1.; **d.** 2.; **e.** 3.

❻ LISTENING • NOTE-TAKING

Tapescript

Wagner: Well, if we do manage to *pull this off*, a lot of the credit will go to your assistant, Julia.

Van der Merwe: Evelyn George? Yes, I know what you mean, we *took a big chance* using her in those technical demos, but she handled it really well. She asked all the toughest questions we could *think up*, and *of course* Narinder was ready *to tackle* all the answers. Anyway, it seems *to have borne fruit*, I mean the response we've had from the police and the insurance companies is not bad *at all*, *on the whole*.

Wagner: Yeah, *it pays dividends to plan ahead*, that's *for sure*. More about that *in a moment*, but *in the meantime* can we do a *checkover* on the results *so far*? Right, so *in a nutshell* we've done all the technical demos for police and insurers and *at least* they're showing a positive interest, but as we all know this is just *a means to an end*, *in terms* of our overall *game plan*. We're *in touch with* the DTI and Saturn about official licences and site-sharing, but *as yet* we've made no move *with regard to* the motor and accessory manufacturers. OK *so far*?

Van der Merwe: Yes, except just one point, we're running *behind schedule*. Up to now it's all been on the development and production side and *as yet* we *haven't got in touch with* our market, and we need *to take steps* to do that *right away*.

Buchan: Umm, I'd *go along with* that, but we haven't really *made enough headway* with the insurance companies and Saturn either. I need *hard facts* and firm figures to *base my final financial projections on*.

Wagner: Yes, I *agree with* you both. So let's *start with* the easy part. I think the response from the police may be enough to get a provisional licence from the DTI. And we need to *tackle* Saturn about *the ins and outs of* site-sharing arrangements. But *in the short term*, we have to get them *to play ball with regard to setting up a dry run* for the insurers and the police.

Van der Merwe: And I don't think we're going to be able to *cut corners* there.

Wagner: Yes, I'm sure you're right, there are no *short cuts* there. But we have *to take care* not to get into an *all or nothing* situation with Saturn. We'll have to *think out* our approach to them very carefully.

Buchan: But surely we can *come up with* some other way of *trying out* the system. I mean, it's a bit of *a long shot* to get *more or less* the whole system *set up* for just *a dummy run*. You see, with respect to you both, it seems a bit of *a snap decision* to me. I suggest we *think it over*, otherwise we'll be *in the red* before we know it.

Wagner: *I take your point*, Norman, but we have to *make progress* somehow, if not we're *caught up in a vicious circle*. And if we don't *make some kind of deal with* Saturn, we *don't even get to first base with* the whole *game plan*. There's *no easy way out we can take* here.

Buchan: Umm, yes, I accept that, *up to a point at least*, *our back's against a wall*, if we're *to go ahead at all*, *that is*. But we have to *keep an eye on* costs. And we can't do that by *trial and error* tactics. So we need to *put together* a package which will *open doors* at Saturn and *in addition* enable us *to go ahead* with them *bit by bit*, that way we don't *stand to make too much of a loss* if the whole scheme *goes dead*. *Better safe than sorry*. *In fact*, I've got an idea *taking shape in that respect* but it needs *thinking out* carefully.

Wagner: OK Norman, if you can *come up with* something concrete it'll be *a big step forward*. So, can we deal with Julia's point about *getting in touch with* the market? Julia, any ideas?

Van der Merwe: Yes, I really feel we need to *be forging ahead with* promoting the product with our main target, *that is*, the motor and accessory manufacturers. *By the way*, I've now got all the statistical information I need *to base* our *game plan on*, so I'd like to *arrange for* a series of presentations, followed up by technical demos, as before, *to break the ice*. And I think we have to *allow for* the fact that *in all probability* they'll want the chance to see *a dummy run as well*.

Buchan: What about price?

Van der Merwe: Well, *of course* that's going to *depend partly on* the outcome of our discussions with the insurers and Saturn, we have *to take that into consideration*, but I was hoping you could help us out on that one *as well*, Norman, if it's not going *to put pressure on* you too much, I know you're busy.

Wagner: I'm sure Norman will *put something together* if he can, Julia. Now, what about the results of your research, can we see what you *came up with*?

❼ COMPREHENSION

a. Evelyn George (Julia Van der Merwe's assistant) attended the technical demonstration. Pretending to be an insurance company representative, she asked Narinder Dhillon the most difficult questions, for which he had the answers ready.

b. Get Saturn *to agree to a dry run* of ASN.

c. *Setting up* the whole ASN system for *a dry run* which *in turn* could mean getting into an *all-or-nothing* situation with Saturn.

d. *Putting together* a package which will *open doors* at Saturn but which will enable Boldmere to *go ahead* gradually.

e. To *get in touch with* the market and promote the product.

f. Presentations and technical demonstrations.

g. This is up to you – we shall see later.

❽ WORD STUDY

a. 6.; **b.** 4.; **c.** 10.; **d.** 13.; **e.** 9.; **f.** 1.; **g.** 3.; **h.** 2.; **i.** 5.; **j.** 7.; **k.** 8.; **l.** 11.; **m.** 12.

❾ WORD STUDY

a. it goes without saying   **e.** in the light of
b. depends on   **f.** on that basis
c. on the lines   **g.** by the same token
d. set out

❿ LISTENING

Tapescript

Receptionist: Saturn, can I help you?

Wagner: Yes, I'd like to speak with Cynthia King.

Receptionist: I'll see if she's free, who shall I say is calling?

Wagner: Jack Wagner of Boldmere.

Receptionist: Just a moment, putting you through.

Cynthia King: Hello Mr Wagner. Cynthia King speaking.

Wagner: Hello Ms King, we had some correspondence not so long ago about site-sharing.

Cynthia King: Yes, I remember, Mr Wagner, what can I do to help you?

Wagner: I'd like to arrange a meeting, to discuss it further, just *in principle* at this stage *of course*.

Cynthia King: We don't do anything *in principle* in this company Mr Wagner, we do things for real. So what have you got in mind?

Wagner: Well, as I think we explained, our company has made what could be an exciting *breakthrough*, but we need *to carry out* tests *to make sure*. It'll . . .

Cynthia King: Sounds interesting. Something in electronics, you said in your letter.

Wagner: Yes, that's right, a new detection system *to be exact*.

Cynthia King: I see, and you want to use us to find out if you really have *broken new ground*, what the *drawbacks* are, if it's *all systems go* or just another *dud*, is that it?

Wagner: Well, yes, *in essence* we need to find out if it's *worth doing* or not.

Cynthia King: So your system's not *for sale as yet* then?

Wagner: No obviously, we need to know we can *make it work*, and that it's going to *pay its way*.

Cynthia King: Mm, let me see if I understand you correctly Mr Wagner, you say you're interested in site-sharing, so you can *try the system out*, using our facilities?

Wagner: Yes.

Cynthia King: I'm not sure that we can help you Mr Wagner. You seem to be looking for some kind of *short-term* arrangement, and I don't see that being to my company's advantage.

Wagner: Mm, I think we may be *at cross purposes. In fact,* we are looking for a *long-term* arrangement. Maybe it'd be better to meet, then I can put our proposals to you *in general terms,* would that suit you?

Cynthia King: All right, I think I can *go along with* that, so when shall we meet? How long do you think you'll need?

Wagner: Mmm, an hour and a half *at the outside,* I should think. Can you be free one day this week or next?

Cynthia King: Mm, mm, hang on a moment, let me just check. I can just fit in a meeting next Tuesday morning, *as long as* it's not too early for you. Is eight-thirty all right?

Wagner: It's never too early to talk business, Ms King...

⑬ READING

overheads costs of running a business
meet to satisfy, to be equal to, *to cope with*
budgets financial forecast plans
due to because of
bad debts debts which cannot be recovered
written off cancelled
diversification variation of products/operations
branching out expansion/diversification
overspending spending over budget
underfunding not enough financial resources
far-reaching wide or extensive in effect/influence

Practice Section E

❶ WARM-UP
You would need to *take into account* the same factors as you would when making a technical demonstration. See the suggestions for Question 1 in the Answer Key for Section D.

❷ LISTENING • COMPREHENSION
Tapescript Part 1
Victor Decard: Well, if you're ready, we're ready.

Van der Merwe: Yes, thank you. As we're all introduced, perhaps I can just start by saying that my company, as you may know, is well established in the electronics field, *in particular, in terms of* security systems. Now, my purpose this morning is to introduce you to an important new product developed by my company. I only need deal *in brief* with the product *as such,* as I shall then hand you over to Narinder Dhillon, our head of R and D, also our Technical Director, who's going to give you a technical demonstration. So I need take only about fifteen minutes *or so* of your time.

Anyway, I'm going to divide my presentation into four short sections. *To start with,* I want to *spotlight* product concepts, features and benefits, things of that nature. After that I want to *throw some light,* very briefly *on* the present situation in the market, then I shall *focus on* market needs, and then finally why we believe that this new product of ours will satisfy that need.

In the course of my presentation I'm going to *refer to* the flip chart, and if you're interested we can let you have copies of the graphics. Stop me at any time if you want to ask questions and I'll try and deal with them but Narinder's the man *to tackle in-depth* questions on the technical side, so you may want to leave those until later.

Right. Every manufacturer has to *cope with* day-to-day problems such as maintaining and improving market share and this, *of course, holds true* for the motor industry, too. Product planners take the basic product, the core product – in your case the motor car – and then add to it, for example style, quality, luxury features *and so on,* often *in the shape of* accessories, including anti-theft devices. *Depending on* the type of product, these can be standard or optional extras, or even bought separately from accessories dealers. With tough competition *to face up to,* it can, and sometimes does, happen that manufacturers *lose touch with* what the market really needs, *that is to say* real benefits, not just luxury features. Now, looking at the chart, Diagram A, you can see ...

Answers to Comprehension Questions
a. 1. Product concepts, features and benefits
  2. The present situation in the market
  3. Market needs
  4. Why Boldmere's product will satisfy market need
b. The market needs real benefits, not just luxury features
c. This is for you to decide

❹ WORDSTUDY
a. to hand over to transfer
b. concepts general ideas

c. **features** aspects of a product

d. **benefits** advantages that a product provides to the consumer

e. **flip chart** a series of charts or diagrams clipped together at the top and fixed to a board, which can be easily turned (flipped), used as a visual aid

f. **core product** the central, basic or essential part of a product

g. **standard** usual, regularised, of the medium or accepted kind

h. **optional extras** features or benefits supplied with a product, *in addition to* those fitted or provided as standard, which a buyer of goods can choose to have, usually at extra cost

i. **dealers** traders, those in the business of buying and selling (usually a specific product type)

❺ LISTENING • COMPREHENSION

Tapescript Part 2

Van der Merwe: No? No questions at this stage. Then it's *a safe bet* that you're wondering why I'm here. Because *at first* you may think that trading conditions *rule out* marketing new products *in general* and a new anti-theft device *in particular. Point taken.* And it's certainly true to say that there are products *of this nature* on the market, *varying from* simple steering wheel locks *to* the lazy lock. *Of course* we have no way of knowing how many vehicle thefts are prevented by these devices. But we do know how many are not. *In a moment* we'll be looking at some statistics *in that respect.* And in a recession, with financial markets in confusion, soaring costs, buyer confidence down and growing stockpiles of unsold products, who wants to take a new product on board *in any case, at least for the time being?* And *of course* the motor industry is *no exception* in thinking *on those lines.*

Well, if it's *a matter of* style or features, then that probably *makes sense. On the other hand,* you may also *agree that* tough times *make it clear* where a company's strengths and weaknesses lie. And it's *in this respect* that a recession is exactly the time when the *go-ahead* companies *take steps* to *get to the bottom of* market problems, *come up with* answers and *zero in on* new opportunities. And one of those opportunities is to *focus on* real benefits to the customer, something the market really needs.

Victor Decard: So what you're saying is that in the good times, when we're all *in the black,*

companies like mine ignore what the market really needs, we *go for soft options,* and as a result we're all *paying the penalty* at the moment, but you've come along *to save the situation* so that we don't have to *take the consequences?*

Van der Merwe: I wouldn't *put it* like that, no not *at all,* that would be overstating my case. But speaking *in general,* when business is good and everyone is *making money* it can be easy to *take the line* of *least resistance in marketing terms.* But when you *run up against* real problems, when you're *competing against* the effects of a recession, it's the *go-ahead* companies, like yours, that turn problems into opportunities, and features into benefits, that's why they survive. I hope that answers your question?

Victor Decard: *More or less* I think. Please go on.

Van der Merwe: Thank you. Well, I now *come to the point.* We did some research and *came up with* some answers, as you can see from the four diagrams I'm now going to show you. Diagram B shows vehicle thefts in the UK, Diagram C is *based on random* sampling among drivers in the Greater London area, while Diagrams D and E *consist of* analysis of information supplied by insurers. I'd like to look at these *in turn in a little more detail in a moment* but, *in a nutshell,* the figures show . . .

Answer to Comprehension Question

A recession makes a company's strengths and weaknesses clear; and *go-ahead* companies use this as a time to identify and resolve problems and *focus on* new opportunities, including *looking into* what the market really needs and offering real benefits to the consumer.

❼ WORD STUDY

a. 7.; **b.** 4.; **c.** 6.; **d.** 10.; **e.** 2.; **f.** 12.; **g.** 11.; **h.** 3.; **i.** 5.; **j.** 8.; **k.** 1.; **l.** 9.; **m.** 13.

❽ LISTENING • COMPREHENSION

Tapescript Part 3

Victor Decard: Yes, I'd like to have copies of the diagrams, we'll put them to our own *acid test,* if we decide we want to take matters further with you.

Van der Merwe: Yes, we can certainly arrange that. Right, turning now to the last section of my presentation. *As we have seen,* there is a clear need for *steps to be taken* to cut vehicle thefts. But this is only *the tip of the iceberg*. Insurance premium rates have risen so sharply that, *according to* our survey, the market, *that is to say* your market, sees these as a serious factor *to be taken into account* when thinking of buying a new car. And the signs are that many people are simply *making do with* what they have. *In addition*, motor insurers are becoming increasingly, er, sceptical *with regard to* vehicle theft claims. *In a word*, many policyholders are making claims *in vain*. This can only reduce buyer confidence still further. Which leads me to one final statistic, the recovery rates for stolen vehicles. If we look at Diagram F, well, I think *the facts speak for themselves*.

Now, to conclude. Taken *as a whole*, the facts suggest that the market needs a new product which will increase buyer confidence, which will be of real benefit and at the same time attract the support, even the active cooperation, of the motor insurers and the police. My company has developed just such a product. *In other words* we have turned a feature into a benefit and *in a moment* you'll be able to see a demonstration. But first, if there are any more questions.

Robert Kerner: Well, we haven't seen your system yet, but *in effect* you're saying that the other anti-theft devices on the market are *duds*.

Van der Merwe: No, but *the facts do speak for themselves*. What the market is getting *falls short of* what it needs. At the moment it's the insurance companies that are *making all the profit*, and it's not only the motorist who's *paying the price*. So if the motor industry can *come up with* an answer, then the insurers may be prepared to *play ball*, and then everyone benefits. And we believe we have the means to *make it work*. *In fact* I think this could now be the right time for Narinder to take over.

Answers to Comprehension Questions

a. She means that the motor manufacturers are also suffering because of falling sales – she has already *referred to* 'stockpiles of unsold products'.

b. The main theme of the presentation is that manufacturers can no longer afford to regard anti-theft devices as luxury features – they should supply these as part of the basic product, as benefits; and that, without openly criticising other devices, the statistics and market survey clearly show a need for an effective anti-theft system, which Boldmere can supply.

⑩ READING
liabilities debts
fall due become payable
stall to delay
due to payable to
call for *insist on*
deadline time limit
overdue late
close down stop/cause to stop operating
end up to finish by
going out of business stopping trading; going bankrupt

Practice section F

❻ TRANSFER • NEGOTIATING PRACTICE
Scenario A: Negotiating Brief for Pietro Cardini representatives*
You must negotiate the best terms for your company, balancing the urgent need to find a new licensee with the knowledge that your company's reputation will ensure you a strong bargaining position.

Before the negotiation, you should decide your overall strategy, and the tactics you will employ to get what you want. You should also make a list of objectives, on a scale from 'must get' (100% necessary) downwards. Also, *in the case of* individual objectives, you should set minimum/maximum acceptable limits. Remember, in all licensing agreements, your company remains responsible for *arranging* and paying *for* marketing and advertising, while supplies of materials for products are the responsibility of the licensee.

You are now to meet the representative(s) of a proposed licensee, Cutlass Fashions.

*If more than one, you should decide what function each of you is to perform.

❶ WARM-UP
A general guide to preparations for negotiation.
1. Set minimum objectives ('must gets') and ideal objectives ('might gets') *in order to plan*

ahead for making tactical concessions.

2. Agree an agenda *at the outset*.

3. *Allow for* the other side's strengths and weaknesses, try to think how they could benefit by *doing a deal with* you – and how they might lose by not doing so – and try to anticipate their tactics so these can be dealt with.

4. Decide your tactics and, if more than one in your team, functions or roles of each team member.

❷ WORD STUDY

a. **to withhold** to keep back, to not give

b. **conservation/green belt area** zone of farmland, parks, open country or natural beauty protected by law from building and industrial development

c. **to ascertain** to find out/*make sure*

d. **approval** formal agreement/favourable opinion

e. **grant** formal giving or consenting

f. **to come to terms with** to reach agreement with

g. **forthcoming** approaching in time; about to happen

h. **feedback** reaction/response

i. **to commit oneself** to enter firmly into a promise, agreement or course of action

j. **measurably** able to be measured

k. **at the end of the day** in the final result

l. **to buy an idea** to accept an idea as true or practical

m. **to look at** to view/think about

n. **manufacture under licence** making a product with formal permission from the owner of the patent

o. **to be with (someone)** 1. to give support/encouragement/approval; 2. to understand

p. **low-key** restrained or subdued

q. **to get the green light** to be given permission

r. **on favourable terms** on advantageous conditions of agreement

s. **phase** a stage in a sequence

t. **to put forward** to propose/suggest

u. **outlay** cost/expense

v. **to up** to increase

w. **to cost** to require heavy outlay

x. **to take the line that** to put forward or follow a particular proposal or suggestion

y. **to work to someone's advantage** to help put someone in a more favourable position

z. **an agenda** list or schedule of items to be dealt with or discussed

❸ LISTENING • NOTE-TAKING • COMPREHENSION

Tapescript Part 1

Van der Merwe: So, *in essence* the feedback from the market is, yes, *on the whole* they're interested *in principle*, but *of course* they're not *as yet* prepared to commit themselves *in case* it all *goes dead*.

Wagner: How do you mean?

Van der Merwe: Well, the same as the insurers and the police; *that is*, they want to *make sure* that ASN is going to work *in practice. First and foremost* they want to be sure that the system isn't *a dud*, that it's not going to *break down every other* day, or *at all in fact*; they want to know they can *rely on* it. Then they can *make their minds up* if it *stands a reasonable chance of* producing results *in the shape of* fewer thefts or *at least* a measurably higher recovery rate for cars *and so on* that do get stolen. And *in order to* do that, we have to give them *a dummy run*. At the end of the day they're looking for a real benefit at reasonable cost to improve buyer confidence.

Buchan: So they bought the idea of ASN as a real benefit, not just a luxury feature?

Van der Merwe: Yes, *as long as* it works *in reality*. But that's just *the first step*. After that, it's *a matter of talking over* price and manufacture.

Wagner: Price, sure, but manufacture's got *nothing to do with* them. That's for us to decide.

Van der Merwe: Yes, I *take your point*, Jack, but some of them I think are already beginning to look at it *in global terms* or not *at all*. They're thinking that it's *not worth their while* fitting ASN to just a few cars, but if the system is successful and can be used *in the future*, and *on a wider scale*, then manufacture abroad under licence could cut costs. But that's the manufacturers – and then only some. And *of course* the accessory dealers *take a different view*.

Buchan: Mm, it's beginning to look as if *to start with* we could be *doing business only with* the accessory dealers.

Van der Merwe: Maybe, but as I said, if we get the price right . . .

Wagner: Yes, and don't forget that if the insurers are with us, then reduced premiums may be a strong incentive for manufacturers to pass on to their own market.

Buchan: Ah, yes, I hadn't *allowed for* that.

Van der Merwe: Yes, and *what's more* I *took care to* be very low-key *in that respect*. So we can still keep that one as a sweetener for the manufacturers, *to soften them up.*

Wagner: OK, good. Julia, you're amazing. You've *opened doors* with the market and *kept our options open as well.* I only hope Norman and I can *make the same kind of headway with* Saturn. *In fact* I'd like to *focus on* that *straight away.*

Answers to Comprehension Questions

a. (i) They are interested *in principle.*

(ii) They want to *make sure* ASN is going to work *in practice*, that they can *rely on* it, that it is likely to *result in* fewer motor thefts or a higher recovery rate for stolen vehicles. All this means that *a dummy run* is necessary. Questions of price and manufacture also remain *to be talked over.*

Tapescript Part 2

Buchan: Yes, you said that they seemed interested, anyway. Who did you speak to?

Wagner: The development manager. Yes, she seemed OK, *up to a point*. But right *from the outset* she took the line that all the advantages are on their side.

Van der Merwe: Mm, so they're going to need *softening up*, otherwise we'll *reach a stalemate* before we get started. Did you put forward the possibility of an option?

Wagner: No, no, much too soon for that. I just gave her *the bare bones* of our plans and needs, nothing more.

Van der Merwe: Uh, that's OK then.

Wagner: Anyway, we've got a meeting *set up* for next Tuesday so we need to *put together* a flexible *game plan* so Norman and Narinder and I go in well prepared and come out with a good result. That's *the aim of the exercise, in any case*, and we'll have Narinder to back us up on the technical side. That way we can avoid anything *going wrong* that needn't *go wrong*. So, can we start with our objectives?

Buchan: But aren't we just *aiming at* getting an option for site-sharing, so we can *go ahead* with *the dry run*? I mean, everything else *depends on* that, doesn't it?

Wagner: Well, yes, but *it's not as simple as that.* We need to get the green light for *a dummy run, for sure*. And at the same time we need to *make*

sure that if the police *and so on* are interested we can *go ahead at will* on the site-sharing, also that if we really do come to *a dead end* we can *back out at once* and *cut our losses*. That's not new, though, that's your idea, Norman. But taking things a step further, if we do *go ahead* we need to *make sure* that site-sharing is on favourable terms and that we do it *bit by bit*, starting with the Greater London area, phase one if you like, then we expand at the same rate as Saturn if all goes well. So we need to negotiate overall terms *in respect of* all phases, but *on the basis that* we *go ahead at will* but that Saturn can't *change their mind* and *withdraw*.

Van der Merwe: So, those are the objectives?

Wagner: Yes, *in broad terms*, if we can *agree on* that, but we need to be more definite, more specific, and separate the 'must gets' from the 'might gets'.

Van der Merwe: Uh? Oh, uh-huh, you mean, like the points we *hold out for* and the ones where we can *back down*, that sort of thing.

Wagner: Yeah, *give and take*. Above all, getting our priorities right.

Buchan: Well, it seems to me that our method of approach is going to be *all-important* here. *On the one hand* we need to show them that we don't *stand to make a massive profit* for only a small outlay. But *on the other hand* that we *mean business*.

Wagner: I'm not with you, can you explain?

Buchan: Well, if they think we *stand to make a lot of money*, they're going to up the price, right?

Wagner: *For sure*, yeah.

Buchan: But if they get the impression that ASN is a bit of a *hit and miss* idea, and they're going to *lose money on* it if the scheme *goes dead*, then, *in all probability* they'll try and make us lose interest by upping the price *in that case as well*.

Van der Merwe: Mm, the main thing is they know that if we *set the system up of our own accord*, it's going to cost.

Buchan: Yes, because of their own level of investment and the *risks they've taken*. But that could work to our advantage. I mean, if we approach them on equal terms, *that is*, taking the line that if it all works out then we'll all be working *in conjunction*, that if they help us, we can help them . . .

Wagner: Yeah, then maybe they'll *play ball.*

129

Mm, we've got the beginnings of a viable *game plan* here, I think. But we're going to have to *take the initiative* though, agree an agenda *at the outset*, and, Norman, you and I are going to have to play different parts, but *hand in hand*, so we need to *think that out* carefully.

Van der Merwe: Yes, and we have to decide whether to put forward our proposals one by one or *as a whole*.

Buchan: Or a series of packages, maybe.

Wagner: Okay, it's beginning to *take shape*. It's getting late again but can we carry on until we've *thrashed it out in detail* . . . ?

❹ WORD STUDY
a. 5.; **b.** 10.; **c.** 9.; **d.** 2.; **e.** 7.; **f.** 6.; **g.** 13.; **h.** 1.; **i.** 3.; **j.** 12.; **k.** 11.; **l.** 4.; **m.** 8.

❻ TRANSFER • NEGOTIATING PRACTICE
Scenario A Negotiating Brief for Cutlass Fashions representatives*
You must negotiate the best possible terms for your company, which:

- is a medium-sized UK clothing manufacturer/distributor;
- has a good reputation as a supplier of quality products;
- last year borrowed a million pounds from the bank to finance a complete modernisation programme, recently completed;
- borrowed the money on the strength of a series of large orders from a chain store which has now gone out of business, causing serious cashflow problems;
- employs a workforce of five hundred in a high unemployment area;
- urgently needs a large, profitable contract *in order to* avoid possible bankruptcy or, certainly, major redundancies.

You are to meet representative(s) of Pietro Cardini, to try and negotiate a licence to manufacture and distribute their products in the UK. Before the negotiation, you should decide your overall strategy and the tactics you will employ to get what you want. You should also make a list of objectives on a scale from 'must get' (100% necessary) downwards. Also, *in the case of* each objective, you should set minimum/maximum acceptable limits. You are particularly concerned to keep profit margins high and royalty payments to a minimum and to negotiate a minimum term of

three years, *in order to* maximise profits, to keep the bank's confidence and to avoid redundancies.

You are now to meet representatives of Pietro Cardini.

*If more than one, you should decide what functions each of you is to perform.

Practice Section G
❶ LISTENING • NOTE-TAKING
Tapescript Part 1
Wagner: Thank you Narinder. As you've just heard, ASN has patent protection. *In addition*, *according to* the DTI, it's *in line with* their own requirements for a code operator's licence, but *of course* you're familiar with all that already yourselves. And *what's more*, the police *go along with* the idea *as well* and that's crucial, as we'll be working *hand in hand* with them. *By the way*, they've seen a technical demo and we are happy with their reaction. And *in any case* if the police *took a different view*, then we wouldn't have *got to first base with* the DTI. But *above all* the fact that we *see eye to eye with* the police *ties in* one hundred per cent *with* our own number one commitment, and *that*, *in a nutshell*, *is* cutting crime.

Cynthia King: We're not exactly against reducing crime either, Mr Wagner, but I take it that you expect *to make a profit*, the same as us?

Wagner: Well, like you, we're an efficient organisation and we're not in business *to make a loss*, that's *for sure*.

Cynthia King: All right, *point taken*, please go on Mr Wagner.

Wagner: Thank you, yes, but I'm happy you raised that point and I'd like to come back to it again later. Anyway, we've also given technical demos to our market, *that is*, the motor manufacturers and the accessory dealers, and we got a good response from them *as well*. Also, the motor insurers . . .

Richard Fromm: Mm, uh, can I just ask how the motor insurers come into this?

Wagner: Yes, *to put you in the picture*, the insurers *take the point* that *on paper* the system could cut vehicle thefts and increase the recovery rate for stolen vehicles. What we're *aiming at* is to get them to see that it's likely to work *in practice*, so they cut premium rates for vehicles fitted with ASN. And *in our opinion* that will help give a boost to the motor market. Which *for the most part* is why the manufacturers like the idea. And, just *in passing*, that could be interesting for you *as well*.

Richard Fromm: I'm not with you.

Wagner: Well, *to put it differently*, more cars could mean more car phones.

Richard Fromm: Mm, it's an interesting point, but . . . mm, okay, carry on.

Wagner: Right, *to come to the point*. We believe we have a viable product. But we have to prove it. To the police, to the insurers, to our market *and so on*. That's *the first step*. After that we consider our options.

Cynthia King: And what are those options?

Wagner: Well, *taking the long view*, *to set up* our own network, that's one possibility. As an alternative, *to tie in with* another network, *as long as* it's suitable for our needs – yours for example.

Richard Fromm: From what Mr Dhillon was saying, then that could be the case.

Wagner: Maybe, but we don't know until we try. If I can *lay it on the line to* you, ideally we'd like to *try out* our system *on a larger scale*, but use your network in Greater London, or part of it, for *a dummy run*. That way we can see *either way* if your network is *in line with* what we need. And at the same time we can show the police *and so on*.

Cynthia King: As Mr Fromm said, we are confident that our network would meet your requirements. And I'm not sure we could *go along with* your suggestion without some kind of *long-term* commitment on your part . . .

Answers to Comprehension Questions

a. Saturn's reaction is that of a company confident of its strong negotiating position, but willing to do business. By questioning the statement that crime reduction is Boldmere's prime target, Saturn issues a challenge to Boldmere's status, with a warning that the negotiation should *focus on* realities. Although it is unnecessary to develop this challenge, Saturn goes on to interrupt with several questions, *aimed at* getting more information. Saturn then goes on to suggest that its network could be suitable for Boldmere's needs, at the same time *making it clear* that

cooperation, *in the shape of a dry run*, will not be considered without a firm commitment from Boldmere.

b. This will become clear in the next section.

❷ WORD STUDY
a. **I take it that** I assume/I suppose
b. **to raise a point** to mention an item or detail
c. **to come into it** to be relevant
d. **to give a boost to** to increase
e. **that could be the case** this may be the real situation
f. **to meet a requirement** to satisfy it

❿ TRANSFER • NEGOTIATING PRACTICE
Scenario B: Negotiating Brief for Pietro Cardini representatives
Your company's position is clear – you blame Cutlass Fashions for the drop in UK sales, *on the grounds of* inferior product quality:
● chemicals used in cloth dyes caused widespread allergic skin reactions;
● use of poor quality materials, *resulted in* shortening of product life;
Both problems have received extensive publicity following complaints from customers. *In addition*, no royalties have been received under the agreement.

Although your company is seriously considering *withdrawing* the licence *from* Cutlass, you recognise the fact that you could *lose face* by continually changing licensees.

You are now to meet with Cutlass Fashions representatives to try and *settle your differences*.

❸ LISTENING • NOTE-TAKING • COMPREHENSION

Tapescript Part 2
Wagner: What do you have in mind?

Cynthia King: Well, *in the first place*, from what we've heard *so far*, linking your system to ours, even for *a dummy run*, is *not going to be as simple as all that*. Especially as it means the police are going to have access to the switching centres. It's going to mean a lot of work. And *what if* something goes wrong with the link-up and our whole system *goes out of action*? We and our customers would be left *to take the consequences*, and those could be serious. I'd like to stress that we *do have an open mind* about your proposition *in general terms*. But we have to protect ourselves and our customers. And I think you'd *agree that* we'd be *falling short of* our obligations if we simply allowed you to come along, *more or less at random*, and *tie your system in with* ours, but with no commitment from you. We'd be *running too great a risk.*

Richard Fromm: Yes, we have to *take a firm line on* that one, Mr Wagner. As Ms King says, we're *open-minded in most respects.* We're happy to talk business with you *on a realistic basis.* But if all you're looking for is to *try out* your system, then I'm sorry but your visit here today may be *in vain.*

Wagner: Mm. But *on the other hand*, we couldn't make any commitment, *at least* not *as yet*, not without a clear *go-ahead* from the police *and so on. In other words*, not without a successful *dummy run.* That would go against all *common sense*, you'd *agree with* that. But going back to what you said just now about *making money.* We believe we can do that, but only by *going ahead bit by bit.* We have to *think carefully ahead.* If we overstep the mark at any stage, then we're *in the red at once* and we and our shareholders *pay the penalty.* But *as a matter of fact*, I'm a bit *taken aback* to hear that *a dummy run* could put you at risk.

Richard Fromm: That's how it is, I'm afraid. It looks like we could be caught up in *a vicious circle* here.

Wagner: Mm, *in that light* . . . uh, Norman.

Buchan: Mm, yes, if I can come in here? I'm not really so sure about that, *at first sight*, yes, maybe we are caught up in a circle but, you see, we could be talking ourselves out of a deal here. Just *to put the record straight*, we seem to be going in the same direction. *In other words*, we each have a system we want to network *on a national scale.* Then if, and only if, the two systems are compatible, it could *make sense* all round for us to make a firm commitment, *as long as* we can *arrange for* safeguards.

Richard Fromm: What kind of safeguards do you mean?

Buchan: Yes, I'll come to that in a moment. But *as we've just seen*, we both *stand to* lose in different ways and for different reasons if we *go ahead on the wrong lines.* But you see *in the same way* we could also both *stand to* lose if we don't *go ahead at all.* And *by the same token* we might both *stand to* gain if we can sort something

out. *The facts really speak for themselves.* The crux of the matter is, are the two systems compatible?

Cynthia King: So what do you suggest?

Buchan: Well, if we can *focus on* the question of safeguards, mutual safeguards, that seems to be the key.

Answers to Comprehension Questions

a. They are willing to negotiate but *insist on* a firm commitment from Boldmere before *agreeing to a dummy run* because of the risks.

b. First he stresses the disadvantages of *going ahead* in the wrong way or not *at all*, secondly he emphasises the advantages of *going ahead* with mutual safeguards, *as long as* the two systems are compatible.

❹ WORD STUDY

a. 7.; **b.** 1.; **c.** 9.; **d.** 2.; **e.** 6.; **f.** 10.; **g.** 3.; **h.** 8.; **i.** 4.; **j.** 5.

❻ LISTENING · NOTE-TAKING

Tapescript Part 3

Richard Fromm: Right, so let's summarise your proposals *so far.* You're suggesting we agree terms for site-sharing in Greater London. But this is not to *take effect* for up to six months and *in the meantime* you want to *arrange for a dry run*, with the option to *withdraw* within the six-month period *in case* you *come up against a dead end.* Am I right *so far*?

Buchan: Yes, and to *make sure* the systems are compatible.

Richard Fromm: Well, I can see how that safeguards you. Anyway, you want to instal your own equipment in part of our Greater London network and *tie in with* it, with the police having access to switching centres.

Buchan: Yes, but you see all this is just for *the dry run.*

Richard Fromm: But Mr Buchan, you mentioned mutual safeguards. So?

Wagner: Yes, any option agreement would *take that into account as well*, guidelines on technical cooperation, to deal with the risks to yourselves.

Richard Fromm: But what about payment?

Buchan: Yes, *of course* we'd be prepared to pay a fee for the option, which you'd keep *in any case*, but to be set off against rental *and so on* if we *go ahead.*

Richard Fromm: I see. And are you going to *keep us in the dark* about this fee, or do you want us to fix a figure?

Buchan: Well I think that has to *depend on* the outcome of the main negotiations. But I had in mind the equivalent of the full six months' rent for the facilities we actually use.

Richard Fromm: I think we'd need to *sleep on that one*, Mr Buchan. Anyway, *all in all* this looks like *a step forward*. But I'm not sure if it will go far enough to meet our requirements. We may need to see a *wider-scale* commitment.

Wagner: What do you mean?

Richard Fromm: Well, for example, an option *on a national scale*. Then we could maybe consider an all-round deal, better for you, better for us.

Wagner: Mm, *in theory* that could be interesting, *other things being equal*, but still premature. We need to *keep our options open* at this stage. For example, *what if* you don't expand your network on a national basis as quickly as we need? If we're tied to a national site-sharing agreement, we can't *take the initiative of our own accord*.

Richard Fromm: Yes, *I take your point*. Well we can *think that one over*.

Wagner: *On the other hand*, if we came to an all-round agreement *based on* a series of phased options ...

Richard Fromm: Well, mm, a possibility. But *as to* site-sharing *in general*, we have *allowed for* that in our development plans. Our lawyers have advised a standard agreement, we can *arrange for* a copy to be sent to you. Unless *of course* you'd like to *talk it over* now?

Wagner: No, I don't think that would be appropriate right now. What we do need are some guidelines on overall costs.

Richard Fromm: Well, *that depends*. We have around fifteen hundred sites, maybe *more or less*, in the Greater London area, and costs *vary from* site *to* site.

Wagner: You'll let us have details of this *as well*?

Richard Fromm: Yes, along with an outline of our national development plans and standard terms.

Wagner: And one final point ...

Richard Fromm: Yes, Mr Wagner.

Wagner: If we do *go ahead*, we'll need to *arrange for* Security Identification Numbers. Also we're going to need some for *a dry run*.

Richard Fromm: That's *no problem at all*.

Wagner: Right. *In that case*, I think we've gone as far as we can *for the time being*. Let's just *check over* the main points again ....

❽ LISTENING · COMPREHENSION

Tapescript

Wagner: Okay, I'm sorry I had to call this meeting at such short notice, but it really is urgent. Anyway, what do you want first, the good news or the bad news? Well, the good news is that we just got the final draft Option Agreement through the mail this morning. And it's *more or less* in order, but, have a look at this. It was in yesterday's newspaper. *Of course* we'll have to *look into it in detail*, but it's clear ...

Answers to Comprehension Questions

a. The final draft Option Agreement arrived in this morning's post and it is more or less in order.

❿ TRANSFER · NEGOTIATING PRACTICE

Scenario B: Negotiating Brief for Cutlass Fashions representatives

Sales of Pietro Cardini products have been falling, due to Pietro Cardini's poor marketing and advertising policy – they have made many promises, few of which were kept. The situation became worse when one very large batch of dyed cotton cloth from a Far Eastern supplier proved faulty, with resulting injuries, complaints and publicity. However, all customers affected have been publicly offered compensation – a refund and a Pietro Cardini voucher. So your company feels it has done its best to put matters right.

Your company feels that Pietro Cardini is not *at all* justified in *withdrawing* the licence and payment of royalties (0.5 million pounds in all) has been withheld to try and force them to a. continue the licence and b. increase marketing and advertising activity.

You are now to meet with Pietro Cardini representatives to try and *settle the differences* between you.

Index